"[Al-Solaylee] reaches back to his parents' history, from Yemen in the 1960s through Beirut, Cairo and then back to Yemen through the Arab Spring, in agonizing, heart-wrenching detail. Along the way, he illuminates the complex struggles and historical moments that have shaped the region, all through his very personal vantage point." —*The Globe and Mail*

"[A] forthright and engaging memoir. A gifted storyteller. . . . Deftly interweaving the personal and the political, and covering more than fifty years of Middle Eastern history, this memoir is anything but nostalgic." —*Quill & Quire*

"Brilliant and utterly mesmerizing. . . . The book is informative and emotionally satisfying and a credit to Al-Solaylee's heart-baring skill. It is enthralling, entertaining and a must-read." —*FAB*

"[A] touching account of a gay man's journey to self-awareness. . . . The story gains in poignancy against the backdrop of a Middle East beset by conflict, economic decline and the rise of political Islam. . . . There's much to commend and like in this book. It's often a joy to read." —*Literary Review of Canada*

"An important and captivating read for those interested in issues of immigration and homophobia in the shifting social and political cultures of the Middle East. It's also an inspiration for those who have changed their lives, or will one day, in order to live more openly with their sexualities." —*Xtra!*

"[A]n inspiring story. . . . Al-Solaylee captures the historical moment in a way that's real and compelling." —*In Toronto*

"Despite its light-hearted tone, this beguiling memoir tells an intensely emotional story of one family's eroded dreams. . . . Unembellished and heartbreaking." —2012 Hilary Weston Writers' Trust Prize jury citation

"A wonderful new book." —*Metro Morning*, CBC Radio

"*Intolerable* is a heartbreaking memoir of a man out of place and time. Tracing the Middle East through the 1980s and '90s, this is a personal coming-out narrative with a difference."
—*The Sun Times* (Owen Sound)

"An astounding read." —*Canada AM*, CTV TV

"A fascinating personal story and a history of a once-liberal family transformed by the politics and turmoil of the Middle East."
—*The Next Chapter*, CBC Radio

"This is [a book] about survival and identity on many levels. The whole story is so singular and unlike any biography I have ever read. I could not put it down." —Macleans.ca

"For anyone interested in the Arab World, for anyone interested in the intellectual formation of a theatre critic and scholar, for anyone interested in gay issues in alternative geographical contexts, this volume is a unique contribution to the field as well as an emotionally powerful read." —*Critical Stages*

"As a beloved son and threatened citizen, Kamal Al-Solaylee tells a deeply rending story of his 'escape' from the toxic chaos of Middle Eastern politics and religious fundamentalism. The still-knotted emotions exposed here are boldly explored yet intensely understated. Here is a courageous personal history, all the more powerful for what it asks of every reader: What would *you* have done?"
—Wayson Choy, author of *All That Matters*

"I don't think you'll find a more painfully honest memoir on the bookshelves." —*Inside the News with Peter Mansbridge*

"This wonderful book is the bittersweet story of a young man who grew up in Cairo and was irresistibly attracted to the freedom of the West— and the story of the sprawling family he left behind. As he journeyed toward a new life in Canada, his beloved mother, brothers and sisters succumbed to an increasingly repressive culture that gradually killed their hopes and dreams. Kamal Al-Solaylee has written a powerful memoir that will lift your spirits and break your heart."
—Margaret Wente, author of *You Can't Say That in Canada*

"Kamal Al-Solaylee has written a beguiling memoir. The story of his family's repeated dislocation and changing relationship with Islam provides a new lens through which to consider the recent upheaval across the Middle East. I've read many books on Islam and the Arab world, but none with the intimacy and emotional weight of this one. *Intolerable* is an immigrant tale, a queer history, a geopolitical lesson, and above all, it's a love story."
—Stephanie Nolen, author of *28: Stories of AIDS in Africa*

INTOLERABLE

A Memoir of Extremes

KAMAL AL-SOLAYLEE

Harper*Perennial*

Published by Harper Perennial, an imprint of HarperCollins Publishers Ltd.

Originally published in Canada by HarperCollins Publishers Ltd
in a hardcover edition: 2012
This Harper Perennial trade paperback edition: 2013

HarperCollins books may be purchased for educational, business, or sales
promotional use through our Special Markets Department.

HarperCollins Publishers Ltd
2 Bloor Street East, 20th Floor
Toronto, Ontario, Canada
M4W 1A8

www.harpercollins.ca

Library and Archives Canada Cataloguing in Publication
Al-Solaylee, Kamal
Intolerable : a memoir of extremes / Kamal Al-Solaylee.

ISBN 978-1-55468-887-6

1. Al-Solaylee, Kamal. 2. Journalists—Canada—Biography.
3. Arab Canadians—Biography. I. Title.
PN4913.A4A3 2013   070.92   C2012-908341-0

Printed and bound in the United States
RRD 9 8 7 6 5 4

To Toronto,
for giving me what I've been looking for:
a home

CONTENTS

INTOLERABLE

INTRODUCTION

I am the son of an illiterate shepherdess who was married off at fourteen and had eleven children by the time she was thirty-three.

My mother, Safia, was born and raised in Hadhramaut, a part of my home country of Yemen that is better known today as the birthplace of the bin Laden clan. When she and my father, Mohamed, were married in the fall of 1945, in the port city of Aden, then a British protectorate, he was fresh off serving a stint in the Allied army and she had just reached puberty mere months before. A year earlier, she once confided to me, she had listened to the radio for the first time in her life and her older sister, Mariam, had talked of something called the cinema. The voice of an Egyptian singer, whom she identified years later as Oum Kalthoum, flowed through the airwaves when she walked past a little makeshift work station in the hills of Hadhramaut. Another Egyptian artist—Anwar Wagdi, Egypt's answer to Gene Kelly—was starring in an early musical melodrama, which she never got to see but had Mariam re-enact several times during their breaks from tending sheep.

Little did Safia know then that her father was waiting for her first period, her first tentative step towards womanhood, to pair her off with the son of a co-worker of his in the civil court where both men served as guards. Safia would always muse about the fact that her father-in-law, Abdullah, kept watch over criminals, since Abdullah himself was a runaway from justice, having killed a man near the northern Yemeni town of Taiz as part of a long-standing tribal vendetta. Indeed, Abdullah ended up in Aden in the early 1910s while on the run from his victim's family. He may have been sixteen or seventeen at the time. There was no way of telling his exact age, as birth certificates didn't exist at that time in Yemen's history. He adopted the name Solaylee—also spelled in English as Sulaili— from a small tribe that offered him shelter on their land near the border that divided what was then North and South Yemen. His family name, and by all rights mine, is Komeath.

On the rooftop of the family building in Aden in 1965, Safia holds me tight while she waits for the laundry to dry. She was an overprotective mother—especially of me, her youngest child.

Kamal Komeath. It would have had a theatrical ring to it, befitting someone who studied Victorian melodrama in England and made a living writing about theatre in Canada. It might even be easier to spell than Al-Solaylee, a last name that I've always hated and spent most of my life enunciating one letter at a time—in English and in Arabic.

There's so much to a name in Arabic culture. Your name aligns you socially and politically with your clan or provides an escape from it. When we lived in Cairo in the 1970s, many of our middle-class Egyptian friends adopted foreign names—Susan, Gigi, Michelle—as aspirations to a Western life. Arab nationalists preferred names that drew on local history: Salah, after Salah-ad-Din, who stood up to the Crusaders; or Gamal, after Egyptian president Gamal Abdel Nasser. *Kamal* itself means perfection, or the person who completes something and gives it the final push towards fulfillment. It's one of the ninety-nine holy names for Allah, although my understanding is that I'm named after Kamal El-Shenawy, the Egyptian matinee idol of the 1940s and '50s, who happened to be my mother's favourite, once she experienced moving pictures for herself many, many years later.

The verb form of my name, *kamael,* means to fill in the gap or complete a story. To try to live up to the many meanings of Kamal, even subconsciously, is an attempt at self-destruction, one meaning at a time. It's a given that I am far from perfect, but to fill in the gap between my life now, as a writer and university professor in Toronto, and that of my parents and my siblings in Yemen is what makes this book a necessity and a daunting task. How can I write of a mother who lived and died without learning to read or write in her native tongue, let alone English, when I went on to earn a Ph.D. in Victorian literature? Is it still a "gap" between my mother and me when the distance is the equivalent of living in different centuries and worlds? I look at family photographs in my Toronto apartment and wonder what Safia would have made of everything around me if she were alive today. She'd be shocked to know how little food I keep in the fridge, or that I'm a vegetarian. She was a consummate cook and never served a meal without two kinds of meat at least. She never thought that fish alone counted as a main course and served meatballs as a side dish to go with it. My apartment, decorated with modernist and minimal furniture and abstract art, would strike her as a work in progress. I can almost hear her say, "I'm sure you'll buy more furniture when you've saved up some money." She associated weight gain with health and prosperity and was anxious when I went on a strict diet and lost thirty pounds between visits to Yemen.

When I last saw her, in 2006, she was far gone into Alzheimer's, but she still found it perplexing that I owned a dog in Toronto. "Get rid of him," she pleaded with me, without ever pronouncing his name. "I could no more get rid of Chester than you could give up one of your children," I responded, knowing that appealing to her sense as a mother could still be effective. She nodded and drifted off into an incoherent story, the details of which I can't remember. To her, dogs were those vicious wild animals that occasionally attacked her sheep and bit her as a young shepherdess, or the dirty, rabid ones that roamed the back streets of Cairo and frightened her children every time they got close. What struck me then was her ability to bridge the gaps between her lives as a young girl, a middle-aged mother and now an elderly woman.

She was a pro at it.

Her entire married life was a desperate and difficult attempt at bridging gaps. In 1949 my father decided to study business in London for a year, leaving her behind with the first three children. She was eighteen. When my dad returned from England and started a business of buying and selling rundown properties—an early local example of flipping, in today's real-estate terms—he had developed a taste for the sophisticated English life. Until weeks before his death, in 1995, he was rarely seen in public without a shirt and tie. Traditional Yemeni clothes—including the *fouta,* a skirt-like lower garment—were strictly for home. He introduced cutlery to a household that enjoyed eating with their hands. Mohamed would often tell us a story of how, after several attempts to get his wife used to a knife and fork, he settled on training her to eat with a spoon—at least when they had company. It was one of several and soon-to-be-growing gaps between my parents. A wife who was illiterate, and still a teenager in years if not life experience, hardly provided the necessary adornment for a businessman with career and social-climbing ambitions. Social standing hadn't counted for much in their parents' lives; as long as a bride was young, virginal and from a good Muslim family the rest hadn't really mattered. He couldn't possibly divorce her, not with three children and a fourth on the way, and not since he seemed genuinely in love with her. As a stopgap, he taught her two English phrases, phonetically, so that if an Englishman—and there were many of them milling about Aden, which was then part of the British Empire—came looking for him, she'd not let him down. "Welcome" was the first and easier of the two to learn. "Just a moment" followed a few days later. It wasn't exactly Henry Higgins and Eliza Doolittle but enough to keep him happy and her out of trouble.

Some of my brothers and sisters would tease my mother for her English "vocabulary" and pronunciation. "What's *wahed* [one] in English?" I'd ask her after my English class in school. She'd stare back blankly and patiently as she continued chopping vegetables or frying enough chicken for ten or eleven mouths. She felt quite comfortable setting herself up as an illiterate woman if that meant the kids could show off their education. That's one mother I remember.

But I also remember Safia walking me home from school in Cairo, in May of 1977. She often did that, because she worried about her youngest child crossing streets by himself. I was about to turn thirteen, a year younger than she was when she got married, and, like many teenage children in Cairo, was discovering Western pop music. My first pop crush was on Olivia Newton-John. Her blond, straight hair and romantic music—now classified as easy listening—captured everything I thought was peaceful and gentle about England or America. A shop window on Tahrir Street, halfway between school and home, displayed a cassette of her album *Come On Over.* The album cover, in a stark blue colour, featured a picture of Newton-John with her head just rising above water. I wanted it. I found it haunting, otherworldly almost. I was fascinated by the idea of a world where a picture like that was the cover of a record, having been used to the static painted images of Arab singers on their albums. I couldn't have it, my mother said, until after my year-end exams. Besides, at three Egyptian pounds (less than fifty cents in today's money), such a purchase would break the household budget. To this day I don't know if she simply recognized the album cover or the words *Olivia, Newton, John,* but a few weeks later, on our way home from my final exam, she took me to a place called Barada, also in Tahrir Street, for shawarma and a chocolate milkshake, then all the craze in Cairo, and a present: a copy of *Come On Over.* I remember not liking the album all that much on first listen—it sounded odd, but I couldn't understand why, something to do with the fact that its mix of folk and country songs was beyond my comprehension and musical taste at the time. I've grown to love the album over the years and have since replaced that (bootleg) cassette with a CD, but I still keep my mother's gift as a memento of time, lives and a family long gone.

Since that summer in 1977 so much has changed in the Middle East and in the life of my family. I see 1977 as a watershed year for the ideals my well-read father and my illiterate mother instilled in their children: tolerance, curiosity, equality, hard work, social mobility. Ours was a secular world where freedom of religion—we had many Christian friends and neighbours in Cairo, and my father did business with Aden's small Jewish community—and religious freedom, on the surface at least, coexisted. Our family had been exiled from Aden as punishment for my father's pro-British sentiments and business interests for exactly a decade. After a few years in Beirut my father had relocated his herd of eleven children to Cairo as a safe haven—and that it certainly was, until about 1977, when the then-largely-underground Muslim Brotherhood resurfaced on Egypt's social and political map and began preaching the gospel of a "return to Islam." A trip by Egypt's President Anwar Sadat to Israel to broker peace only strengthened the resolve of Islamists in Cairo to make their philosophy heard and practised. Around the same time, our school, a private co-ed institution for Cairo's middle-class families, hired its first veiled female teacher. Even at thirteen and fourteen, I, like many of my Egyptian friends and other Arab expatriates at Education Home school in Dokki, Cairo, knew something was changing. When Miss Afaf tried to convert female students into wearing the hijab, a parental revolt followed.

Closer to home, my brother Helmi, then in his early twenties, fell under the spell of the Brotherhood and began to scold my sisters for not wearing the hijab, for dyeing their hair or wearing too much makeup. Three of my older sisters had finished university or secretarial schools and were working in foreign embassies, ad agencies and antiques shops. Most people find the ritual of getting ready for work—what to wear, what to pack for lunch—a chore, but my sisters endured it to the soundtrack of a brother barraging them with sayings from the Prophet Mohamed or one of the imams Helmi was in the habit of listening to. He urged them to renounce vanity and cover up their hair. I don't know how my sisters coped with this daily intimidation. My dad worked abroad for most of that time and his secular influence at home was waning.

Perhaps Helmi was trying to prepare my sisters for their future lives in Yemen, our homeland, where the family gradually retreated in the mid-1980s to escape political tensions in Cairo and to settle somewhere after nearly twenty years as expatriates. To my father there was no choice but to return to Yemen. Not the southern port of Aden, where he had found his fortune and started his family, but the northern city of Sana'a, which was slowly making contact with the outside world after decades of an insular, caste-based pseudo monarchy. (The northern part of Yemen became a republic in 1962 and united with the south in 1990 to form the Yemen of today.)

Sana'a? That medieval-looking city we knew only from travel books and poorly shot postcards that relatives sent us on special occasions? I knew instantly that I had to avoid spending the rest of my life in a place where public hangings were held in broad daylight as part of sharia law. I had come out to myself as a gay man and was embracing a Western version of gay identity. Although I joined my family in Sana'a for over a year—serving the mandatory military service, albeit as an interpreter in the central security forces—I was determined not to make Yemen my home and started a journey that would take me to the United Kingdom as a student and to Canada as a landed immigrant.

Some of the details of my own journey I have been able to describe with a certain ease in the chapters that follow. I was able to build on my good education in Cairo all the way to a doctorate in English in the UK and then make a new life for myself in Toronto not long after landing here in 1996. That part is straightforward enough. What happened to my family in the intervening decades is a story I have struggled to understand, explain and put into words. How do you write about, rationalize and call your own a family that still believes AIDS is a form of divine retribution and that men are superior to—and have the right to rule over—women, when you have no problem describing people who espouse similar views as bigots?

My first visit back to Yemen after moving to Canada in 1996 was in the summer of 2001. I found a family that acted a lot closer to the stereotype of regressive Muslim culture than the secular one I'd known. The veils were in full view. Everybody prayed five times a day. My brothers were unapologetically sexist in their dealings with their wives, hushing them whenever they expressed an opinion or telling me not to listen to them. "Women's talk," my brother Khairy said dismissively when his wife complained about life in Sana'a. Was this the same family that passed around the great works of literature and subscribed to several newspapers, three dailies in Arabic and one weekly in English?

The same brother who told his wife not to contribute to the conversation—himself once an M.B.A. candidate—was suggesting that his eldest daughter need not go to university because it wouldn't help her much as a housewife. A sister who worked as a librarian at Sana'a University wore the full niqab, covering all her face except her eyes. When I visited again in 2006, she followed me around town for half an hour, just for fun, without revealing her identity to me. I never noticed or recognized her.

Collectively, they'd become TV addicts. Satellite TV, featuring hundreds of channels from the Arab world, Iran and beyond, had taken over from reading, socializing and going out as the main forms of entertainment. It turned my family from well-educated, intellectual stock into the worst kind of couch zombies. Why? In part because among the many channels they tuned in to were the more Islamist ones (Al-Manar TV of Hezbollah, for example) that promoted a rigid version of the faith. By 2006, anti-Western and pro-Islamist sympathies had intruded on virtually their every conversation with friends, neighbours and each other. They had accepted a need to return to Islam and away from the outside world—an acceptance that had been building slowly for over two decades and claimed even once-progressive families like mine.

But is all that about to change? If so, at what cost and how fast? When I started writing this book, in the fall of 2010, the thought of a people's revolution in Tunisia or Egypt, a military uprising in Libya or a copycat public revolt in Yemen—and all happening either simultaneously or in quick succession—would have been the stuff of fiction. When I visited Cairo in May of 2010, I thought Hosni Mubarak's hold on power was as strong as it had been when I last lived there, in 1986. His crudely painted portraits and ridiculously airbrushed photographs still greeted travellers and commuters in Heliopolis, the suburb nearest the airport, where his presidential palace stood (and where a year later he was facing trial for corruption and ordering the mass killing of protestors). There was no mistaking the profound level of anger and frustration at the poverty, inequality and unemployment that my own sister—who still lives in Cairo—and her circle of friends shared with me. Cab drivers, old family friends and, when prodded, shopkeepers and hotel staff vented all too readily about the Mubarak regime. I witnessed a few protests outside downtown courthouses and saw banners calling for solidarity with silenced journalists or locked-out workers. But at no point did I hear any talk of a revolution, overthrow of government or an uprising, which made the images of Tahrir Square that I saw on TV from my safe Toronto home all the more unbelievable.

I'd walked the same square thousands of times as a child, teenager and young man and returned to it as a middle-aged Canadian at least twice since. During a twenty-four-hour stop in 2006, I gave up on a plan to visit the Egyptian Museum when I couldn't cross the main street that cuts across one part of the square. The traffic had become that chaotic and frightening. But in the winter of 2011 a different kind of chaos was unfolding in the square. It's still unfolding, of course, and no one knows how it will all work out for the average Egyptian, who has to survive on what I probably pay each month for my dog's food and treats. I'm not optimistic. The protestors in Cairo and Western politicians and media have built up expectations of the Arab Spring that can't be met in a few months, years or even a decade of post-revolutionary reforms. The economic disparities in Egypt took more than four decades to accumulate, during which time the population nearly doubled. The life of my own sister illustrates the stagnation in middle-class incomes and the explosion in birth rates and immigration into Cairo.

Farida married an Egyptian in 1980 and still lives in the same rented two-bedroom apartment with her now-retired husband and two children in their early thirties and mid-twenties. When she first moved into that apartment, their stretch of Soudan Street used to be virtually deserted at night. It was too far from her friends and family, my sister would often complain. Taxi drivers refused to go there late at night because there would be no chance of picking up a new fare for miles on the way back. But it was quiet and, all things considered, a safe and family-friendly street. By 2010 it had turned into a main thoroughfare, with new apartment buildings practically attached to each other and round-the-clock traffic jams and noise.

I can't imagine the kind of pressure my first extended visit to Cairo in 2010 must have put on Farida's budget, as she insisted on having me over for lunch at her place almost every day. My niece was now an English teacher in the same school where she (and I) once studied, and my nephew worked for a French bank. And yet what they made was literally barely enough to keep the roof over their heads. The building was by then over thirty years old and a casual observer could instantly spot the flaws in the structure and plumbing. I remembered how many buildings in Cairo were shoddily built in the 1970s and would collapse, sometimes with residents inside them. In fact, we lived near one such building and had to evacuate our own for a few weeks while engineers checked for any structural damage. I was racked with guilt at the financial pressure I was causing and tried to at least pay for the food, whereupon Farida cried from pride and embarrassment. I insisted on giving her two hundred US dollars as a thank-you, for which she was grateful and, eventually, was forced to accept.

Since the start of 2011, I've called Farida every few weeks to check in on her and to see how she has been living in the new, revolutionary Cairo. "Same old," she'll say, "only less safe than it used to be." She tells me stories of thugs—*baltagia*—intimidating average citizens at night and carjacking in once-peaceful residential parts of Cairo. It was alleged that the Mubarak regime released them from prison in the early days and weeks of the revolution in order to intimidate and beat up the protestors. They remain on the loose.

That said, Farida has it easy. Egypt can fall back on a long tradition of civic institutions to protect rights and personal belongings. Despite all Mubarak's oppressive policies, many Egyptians continued to believe in their right to a free and democratic society. The rest of my family in Sana'a wasn't quite as lucky. Not long after the revolution in Egypt and Tunisia (and the protests in Bahrain), thousands of Yemeni citizens of different ages and social backgrounds took to the streets in Sana'a, Aden and Taiz, Yemen's three largest cities, to demand, among other items on a long list of reforms, the ouster of President Ali Abdullah Saleh. He had been in power for over thirty years. (He eventually stepped down in early 2012.) The protests started peacefully enough in the winter of 2011, and the revolutionaries saw Saleh's pledge not to seek re-election in 2013 as a positive sign of an impending change. But by March events took a tragic turn when pro-government forces opened fire and killed almost fifty protestors outside Sana'a University, which had become Yemen's version of Tahrir Square—a tent city where protestors ate, chewed khat, slept, prayed and demonstrated. It's also where my sister Raja'a works as a librarian.

Getting to her office on campus has never been easy for Raja'a, one of my eight siblings who live in Sana'a, along with, at last count, my twelve nephews and nieces. This divorced single mother of my twenty-four-year-old niece daily navigates the city's traffic-light-free streets, crowded *dababs* (minibuses) and airport-style check-points at the university gates. Once throngs of youths had turned the campus and its surroundings into the nerve centre of their revolution, her commute became dangerous as well as difficult. "I used a roundabout, back-of-back-streets path," she told me on the phone during one of our now-weekly checkup calls. That was in March of 2011. By early June, a full civil war had erupted right in the downtown core—less than a mile from our family home in Sana'a's Ring Road—between Saleh's Republican Guard and a rag-tag of tribal militia led by Major General Ali Mohsen, the highest-ranking army officer to support the protesters and add his loyal forces to their cause. For the first time ever, my sisters and my niece, who still lived in the family home, had to leave it behind and seek shelter with siblings and cousins who lived outside the city centre. They returned home only in late June, even as daily skirmishes continued and the sounds of gunfire or explosives could be heard in the distance. It's amazing what you get used to, my sisters told me on the phone. Later in June, Saleh escaped an assassination attempt but was flown into Saudi Arabia for treatment, leaving the country in shambles and, for once, living up to its international reputation as a failed state. Electricity was limited to a few hours a day, and everything from gas to food to water doubled in price in a matter of weeks. Saleh's sudden return in September plunged the country into a second round of civil war.

As I followed news of the stalemate between protestors and government forces from the comfort of my Toronto condo, I understood, even sympathized with, the anger that fuelled it. Since he seized power in 1978 over what was then the Yemen Arab Republic in the north, President Ali Abdullah Saleh has followed the "Blueprint for Arab Dictators" to the letter. He defused pro-democracy sentiments by presiding over a largely symbolic parliamentary system while cracking down on political dissent and placing family members in key government positions. In early 1987 I worked for a few months as a translator for Saleh's brother, Mohammed, who ran the internal security apparatus. Six days a week, I translated and responded to private business letters and proposals from European investors—and the odd arms dealer.

The Saleh clan ran the country like a private venture fund. International aid money, intended to better the lives of the country's now 24.3 million citizens, found its way into the president's inner circle, while the infrastructure of Sana'a—let alone smaller cities and villages—crumbled. Despite some modest oil revenues, inflation and unemployment made daily life almost impossible in a country where over 45 percent of the population survives on less than two dollars a day.

Yemenis have long been the butt of jokes in the Arab world, but they've adapted smartly to water shortages and daily blackouts. My sister Hoda—an executive assistant with nearly thirty years' experience, who late last year secured a low-paying job after eighteen months of unemployment—spends much of her spare time negotiating lower water rates with the private sellers who drive up and down the streets of Sana'a with water tanks. Khairy, a soccer fanatic and father of four, invested in his second electric generator, just in time for the 2010 World Cup.

The 2011 uprising in Yemen and the civil wars that followed have made Yemenis' lives more miserable and are more likely to leave the country devastated than improved economically. Perhaps that's why I have mixed feelings about the so-called Arab Spring, which, a year into it, could stand some revisionist history—at the very least more realistic expectations from everyone there and beyond.

In the midst of all the celebration and suffering in the Arab world today, I want to step back and tell the story of how we got to this boiling point. How did we get from the promise of the post-colonial liberationist era of Nasser, to the dictatorships and social decline of Mubarak in Egypt, Gadhafi in Libya and Saleh in Yemen, to this new liberation movement? Perhaps the journeys that my family and I took weren't always in opposite directions from each other. In committing parts of this story to print, I hope to understand what happened before and during my lifetime to my Arab clan of Al-Solaylee. So much of Arab and Middle Eastern history has travelled through their veins and mine. Maybe I'm trying to live up to my name with the perfectly representative story, if not the perfect representation of a story. And maybe I'm just trying to fill in the gaps, not just between one family, but between the Arab and Western worlds.

I don't know when, how or if the changes in the Arab world will end, but I know that my story begins in Aden.

CHAPTER ONE

ADEN

Camelot

Everything I heard about Aden from my parents made it sound like a place I'd missed out on by being born too late. My older siblings—all ten of them—spoke of it in an equally glowing tone. Forget New York and fly over London; Aden was the place to be, family lore would have me believe. It all came to a violent end in 1967, when the wave of decolonization spreading throughout the Arab world and beyond reached Aden. The Brits were out, the nationalist socialists in and the party over.

I was just over three years old when we left and remembered nothing of it. Such was my father's love for Aden that he would repeatedly ask me as a child if I recalled anything, anything at all, about those first three years. "How could you not remember?" he asked, over and over, teasingly but impatiently. "Leave him alone," my mother would say, and park me back in front of the TV or at my desk. I perfected that rescue-me look and she often responded just in time. It probably wasn't the city itself—its streets, ports or even the people—that Mohamed wished I'd remember but his life as one of its most powerful and influential businessmen. It was a far cry from the severely depressed, beaten-down middle-aged man who for thirty years after our exile kept trying and failing to come close to his glory days in Aden in the 1950s and '60s.

I wish I'd known that father and that Aden. History books tell a more complicated and less rosy story about the city, but as so much of my family's experience was documented in photographs where everyone looked so happy and healthy, I'm siding with the Al-Solaylee version of this Camelot.

The youngest six children on an outing in the Port of Aden in 1966. (Left to right: Hanna, Wahbi, Raja'a, Khairy, Hoda and me.)

This little port city at the southern tip of the Arabian Peninsula became a safe haven for trade and an early colonial melting pot. The British administered it, the Indians lived within it, the Jews felt safe on its lands and Yemenis like my father saw opportunities for business and for family life. I'd say family and money were Mohamed's main preoccupations, except that as a rich and handsome young man, he was also a certified womanizer. My uncle Oubad, my father's youngest brother, often talked to me and my three brothers—these stories, he thought, were not for my sisters—of my father's philandering ways. "The things your father has done! Your mother is a saint for forgiving him," Oubad prefaced every tale. The stories ran along similar lines: Mohamed escaping over rooftops and through back alleys to avoid getting caught in flagrante by a paramour's father or, in some cases, husband. Or Father inviting unsuspecting females to his office to show off the plans for his next development. My favourite, because of its *Mad Men* sordidness (or is it glamour?), my father flirting with flight attendants on the local airline, skyborne and on the ground. Aden was the Monte Carlo of the Arabian Sea, and Mohamed was its Cary Grant. Growing up in Beirut and then Cairo, two cities I know and remember well, I could still see traces of the dapper ladies' man in my father.

Right up to his last few weeks, in fact. As a last chance to stem the spread of cancer in his lungs, Mohamed travelled to England in 1995 for private treatment in Liverpool, where one of my sisters was living. I was still writing my doctoral thesis and commuted between Nottingham and Liverpool to spend time with him. He charmed the ladies even on his hospital bed. He knew there'd be female nurses in hospital and came prepared; he brought ties in dazzling quantity with him to England because he didn't want to look underdressed (or poor) without a healthy rotation of them. He never made a will, even though he knew he was dying, but he made every effort to look good. I'm an out and proud gay man, but there was something about my father's last gasp of heterosexuality and harmless flirting that I found appealing, even romantic. I never told my mother, of course.

It was fitting that his last act of gallantry took place in England. His awareness of himself as a virile young man came about in

London in the late 1940s, when he left Aden, his wife and his three children for a year-long training in business. (Four decades later I'd follow a similar path to England, but for different reasons and outcomes.) He'd tell us about taking room and board near Marble Arch and having a close but undefined relationship with his landlady. My older brother Helmi found these stories unsavoury and didn't trust their accuracy. We probably have some mixed-race brothers or sisters in London, Helmi would say disapprovingly. If only, I'd tell myself. I loved my father's stories and wanted them to be true. Before my first trip to England in 1984, that country and its culture—from Charles Dickens novels to Cliff Richard songs—evoked nothing but romantic associations in my mind. That my father was part of that romantic tradition was all a young boy in Cairo of the early 1970s wanted to hear.

I also knew how Mohamed loved my mother. Yes, theirs was an arranged marriage that would now be illegal in most parts of the world, since the bride had just turned fourteen, but somehow they survived fifty years, eleven children, four countries and a decade-long estrangement later in their lives. As Safia stayed home and cranked out children, Mohamed turned real-estate flipping into a viable business for the first time in Aden's relatively short municipal history. He would either renovate or build lowrises, add storefronts and rent out every last square foot to the local business community or the British and Indian civil servants whose job it was to manage Aden. He was a businessman through and through, so when his own brother wanted to open a small business in one of his buildings, he charged him full rent—including a deposit. No wonder my siblings and I always sensed some resentment from our uncles towards their brother. My mother told me that they refused to take his hand-me-down clothes on principle, and in later years, when Safia or Mohamed was in a more sombre mood, they talked about how the uncles secretly relished his financial fall from grace.

I have a more realistic and sympathetic view of my father after talking about him more with my siblings. He wasn't a ruthless man by any means, but he protected his business interests with a certain ferocity. The very nature of his livelihood depended on gentrifying and building on top of old houses, which inevitably meant buying out or simply evicting long-term residents. He did his best to find them suitable alternatives, but he cared nothing for their emotional attachment to place. Homes—aside from his own—were businesses and he liked to keep sentimentality at bay.

Mohamed was by nature a collector, of real estate, women and children. The thing he wanted most from Safia, however, was a male child. She let him down four times in a row. My mother gave birth to four girls: Fathia in 1946, Faiza in 1947, Farida in 1949 and Ferial in 1951. Their names all started with an *F*, as Mohamed admired the women in the Egyptian royal family of King Farouk, all of whose names started with that same letter. His own mother, Bahga, a Yemeni of distant Indian roots, thought Safia was the problem and began matchmaking for her son, doing the rounds of respectable families to check out potential new brides. I don't think Safia ever forgave her mother-in-law for that, and the relationship between the two of them remained frosty and occasionally hostile until my grandmother's death in 1977. For one thing, Bahga, who had very fair skin, never liked that her equally fair son had married a woman with such a dark complexion. She was determined that Wife Number Two would be *bayda* (white). But just as Mohamed was considering his mother's suggestion of taking on a second wife, who might give him the male heir he wanted so much, Safia finally gave birth to a boy. Mohamed was so overwhelmed he broke the *F* monopoly and called him Helmi, Arabic for "my dream."

But any dreams of adding a second male child to secure an heir and a spare to his little kingdom were shattered with the next three births, all girls. After Helmi in 1953, there was Hoda in 1955, Hanna in 1957 and Raja'a in 1959. It looked like Helmi, already a spoiled brat by all accounts, was destined to be the only male child. By early 1960, Safia was twenty-eight and Mohamed thirty-four. They had eight children. It's staggering to think of a couple so young caring for so many children, even with the extended families of both nearby to lend a hand. I often marvel at my parents' patience and determination when I, at forty-seven, struggle with the responsibilities of looking after one dog—a docile cocker spaniel.

Eight was not enough. Not in the Aden of the 1960s, where my father more or less dominated in business. In less than four years my mother had three more children, and to the infinite delight of my father all were boys: Wahbi in 1960, Khairy in 1962 and me, the youngest, in 1964, making my family the Yemeni equivalent of the original baby-boomer generation, born between 1946 and 1964. My name, Kamal, makes more sense in this context. I was the one to complete the collection of progeny, to bring this child-factory story to its conclusion.

It just so happens that I was born on the afternoon of the Fourth of July. My father claims to have skipped a reception at the American consulate to make it in time for my birth at a small hospital in the Tawahi district of Aden. He repeated the same story every year on my birthday. And every year my mother would repeat—though not to his face—that he was not ever really invited but bothered everyone for an invitation so much they let him attend. By the eleventh child, it was too dangerous for my weakened mother to give birth at home with the help of a midwife, as she had with her first eight or nine children. She had so many deliveries that accounts of our births got fuzzy in her head. My sister Faiza knew for sure that I was born in a hospital. She said she carried me home while my parents and older siblings walked behind her. Faiza would have been just two months shy of her seventeenth birthday and barely out of the convent school in the Badri district of Aden in which she and the three other *F*s were enrolled. I was to be her child, so to speak, partly so she could train for her future and inevitable role as a mother, just as my oldest sister, Fathia, looked after Wahbi when he was born and my sister Farida tended Khairy.

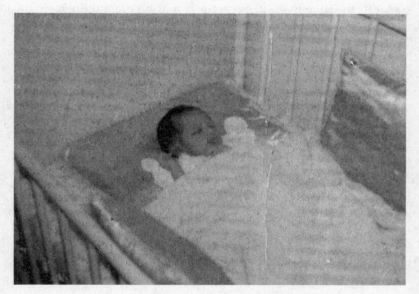

My family's first picture of me, taken in our Aden home in July 1964.

To the harried parents of today, in Yemen or in the West, this arrangement may sound like the best of both worlds, but it often created tensions between my mother and her older children. Faiza and my mother often competed for my affection as a child and teenager, in part because Faiza was never able to conceive during her two marriages. But to me, there was never any real competition. I was Mama's boy. In fact the Arabic phrase *dalo'o omo* (his mother's spoiled child) became my nickname. In public. My own father called me that in front of friends and neighbours—not to tease me so much as to divert any blame that might have come his way for raising an identifiably weak and sports-averse boy who loved watching his mother in the kitchen. Later, even my mother would discourage my too-regular kitchen visits, as if she feared that keeping her company would turn me gay. "The kitchen is no place for real men," she said repeatedly, but she ultimately caved in to my requests to stay put—usually on the condition that I didn't prepare, or get involved in, any food. Her fear of my turning out gay came true, but she needn't have worried about my kitchen skills. I remain a lousy cook with an intense dislike of doing anything in the kitchen other than making tea or toast. My brothers all feel the same way.

It's hard to believe, but in between bringing children into the world and building new apartment blocks, Safia and Mohamed liked to go on holidays with the whole family. In the 1960s, when air travel became more widespread and relatively affordable, my parents would take the whole family (and assorted aunts to help with the younger children) for month-long trips to Cairo, then and now the centre of the Arab world. While I was too young to remember these trips, an extended visual record of them hangs on the walls of my Toronto home. These photographs were my father's way of documenting his success for any doubters. The snapshots serve a different purpose for me, as they're my way to prove to the world (or at least visitors) that there was once a great cosmopolitan and curious Yemeni society that is very different from the images we see in the media of khat-chewing, gun-carrying tribesmen and burka-wearing women.

The three big trips (in 1963, 1965 and 1966) have become the stuff of legend in my family, partly because of logistics. Imagine booking airline tickets for around fifteen family members, renting one or two large apartments in downtown Cairo and making plans to keep children who ranged from young women to toddlers happy and busy for a whole month. And calling that a vacation.

The entire family and two cab drivers (far right) in an Egyptian nightclub before a concert by the singer Abdel Halim Hafez in 1965 or 1966. I'm seated on my mother's lap, of course (second from the left).

My mother was still expected to cook at least one meal a day during these so-called holidays. Whether in Cairo or back in Aden, she never liked servants to help with food preparation for her family and limited their role in the kitchen to cleaning dishes or scouring pots and pans. When not visiting parks, the zoo or going to the movies, my sisters would spend most of the day shopping for clothes. Most Arabs considered Cairo the Paris of the Middle East when it came to fashion, and nowhere was more fashionable than its downtown core, especially a little market named after its red marble floors: the Red Corridor (Mamar el Ahmar). A couple of stores there just sold fabrics, which my sisters (and mother) bought by the yard and had turned into dresses by seamstresses in nearby apartments. You dropped off the fabric on a Monday, selected the design from a pile of Egyptian fashion magazines, went back on Wednesday for a fitting (in Arabic, you use the same word for rehearsal, *prova*) and picked up the dress by Thursday afternoon—just in time for one of the big concerts by such Egyptian singers as Abdel Halim Hafez. By the time we moved to Cairo in 1971, that market had lost much of its glamour but remained our first stop for the annual back-to-school shopping trips.

The choice of Cairo as a summer destination for a Yemeni family was an obvious but emotionally complicated one for Mohamed. By the early 1960s, Gamal Abdel Nasser, Egypt's nationalist president and leader of the Free Officers Movement, which in 1952 had ousted the royal family and ended British rule in Egypt, was busy importing revolutions to other parts of the Arab world. The nationalist, anticolonial movements sweeping the Arab world—a clear predecessor of the revolutions of 2011—posed a real threat to my father. His real-estate empire was built on Aden's stability as a gateway port city open to business and trade, with the British keeping order. He was invested in empire as a commercial enterprise and as a way of life. Nasser's agenda came to fruition in the northern parts of Yemen in 1962, when his troops toppled the ruling monarchy and helped create a republic in the shape of Egypt. It was just a matter of time before the same Arab socialist sentiments would spread south to Aden. Still, Mohamed loved, in theory, the nationalist rhetoric of Nasser, and as with many Arabs, Nasser's role in the frontline against Israel made him a sympathetic figure even to those who stood to lose it all to his politics. Egyptian popular music from the likes of Shadia, Oum Kalthoum, Abdel Halim Hafez and Mohamed Abdel Wahab glorified Nasser and his steadfast position against Western influences. Most of that music was banned during the Sadat and Mubarak years when I was growing up, but now the songs that moved a whole generation of Egyptians are there for anyone to hear on YouTube.

After a number of skirmishes and small-scale protests, the situation in Aden escalated in December 1963 when a group of North Yemen–backed rebels threw a grenade at largely unarmed British officials. The action started what would become known as the Aden Emergency. According to several historians, the British recognized that their time was up in Aden, as vital as that port city was to trade, and whatever was left of the British Empire in the neighbouring Gulf states. So while the Royal Air Force maintained a state of preparedness, diplomats sought other divestment solutions, including declaring Aden and the southern regions of Yemen part of the larger Federation of the Arab Emirates of the South. That solution didn't fly with the two now-competing nationalist factions in Aden: the National Liberation Front (NLF) and the Front for the Liberation of South Yemen, which had the unfortunate *Sesame Street*–appropriate acronym of FLOSY.

Neither ranked particularly high on Mohamed's wish list for a post-colonial Aden. But whether out of blind faith in the British or social prejudice against the largely working-class makeup of both liberation movements, Mohamed did little to prepare for the coming change. In 1965 he built his biggest and most luxurious apartment building—named Al-Azhar, not after the famous Egyptian mosque or university, but because the word means "flowers"—to the cost of roughly a million pounds sterling in today's money. "The British will not let us down," he told my oldest brother, Helmi, groomed from a young age to take over his business. It was around that time, my siblings tell me, that my father developed a lifelong dependence on the BBC World Service. He'd hush down everyone and listen intently to the news, teasing out every last meaning from what he heard. He often switched off the radio to his own announcement that we'd all be all right and that the new building would include an even bigger space for us. He'd hide from his wife and children any intimidating encounter with the young revolutionaries or the odd graffiti message scrawled on his storefronts that described him as traitor. The Brits would come to his rescue. Didn't he speak English just as well as they did?

It was probably that final apartment building, that last act of defiance and faith in Aden as a colonial haven, that pitted the nationalists against Mohamed. We were one of several well-to-do clans, and other business people like my father were harassed, but for some reason my father's presence in the city through real estate made him the kind of public enemy every nationalist movement needs as a target.

The beginning of the end came in 1967. By then infighting between NLF and FLOSY had reached the residential streets of Aden, while attacks on the British military bases and on civil servants continued. Nasser's disastrous performance in the Six Day War against Israel in the same year did nothing to weaken his grip on the liberation movements, least of all in Aden. By November Britain started pulling out its troops from Aden, tacitly endorsing the NLF as the winner of the sectarian war and the new custodian of the city.

How could Mohamed not have predicted that his days, like those of the Brits, were numbered? I still don't know the answer to that question, which haunted my father until his death. "There was nothing I could have done," he often told us, as if to apologize for the fact that as soon as the NLF took power they confiscated all his properties. Five apartment buildings, two houses and numerous storefronts were all now in the possession of the socialist government. There was one thing that my dad held on to for dear life for the next three decades: a leather briefcase that contained the deeds to every last property he once owned. With the reunification of the north and south of Yemen in 1990, a shotgun wedding to avoid bloodshed over newly discovered oil wells, my father lived to see most of his properties restored to him or received token compensation for ones that were literally beyond repair. "Now you see why I held on to those deeds," he'd say triumphantly.

But my father's most frightening encounter with the NLF took place in November 1967, when a small masked group kidnapped him from his office, gangster-style, and held him hostage for thirty-six hours. My siblings and I grew up on several renditions of the kidnapping story. For years it was a story Mohamed would tell guests over dinner in Beirut and Cairo. It's hard to reconcile the different details, but the broad strokes remained the same. "I was tied to a chair,"—that much he always kept consistent. "I asked for a cigarette." I believed that one as well, as he was a compulsive smoker until he quit in 1972. "Their faces were the picture of envy," he'd say of his kidnappers, who took off their masks as an act of defiance. He claimed not to have recognized any of them, although in all probability, my mother would say, some were former contactors who worked for him and resented his hubris. The ransom amount went up or down, depending on who was listening to the story, but it was a few thousand pounds.

One thing was incontestable. Mohamed was given less than a day to leave Aden. Imagine having to find a new home in a new country for a large family (and other dependants) in less than a day. Imagine leaving everything you own and everyone you know and not knowing if you'll ever see them again. I've always felt lucky to have been too young to understand what tearing a family away from their homeland meant. The financial loss was enormous, but the emotional one incalculable. In Beirut and later in Cairo, I grew up watching my father in the grip of what I now recognize as severe depression. By 1972 he was still so traumatized by his losses that he became too sick to see a psychiatrist. The family doctor would visit him in his room and the door would be locked for hours. The TV and radio sets got switched off and we all milled about quietly until that door opened again. Sometimes it was just the doctor asking for more tea or a glass of water, which one of my sisters hurriedly supplied, and further waiting would follow. At other times, Mohamed would sit on the balcony of our Cairo apartment overlooking Tahrir Street and watch the world going by without saying a word to any of us for hours. He'd break his silence only if we had guests.

For my older sisters, the exile from Aden meant the end of their lives as young rich girls. It would be more of a social than a psychological adjustment, the first of many in their lives. It seemed that my father's royal pretentions—manifested in naming four of his daughters in the style of the Egyptian monarchy—may have rubbed off on them. They had every right to think of themselves as princesses. Didn't their father reign over Aden? They had their dresses made in Cairo and bought fine jewellery from the Indian and Jewish traders in Aden. Whether it was Arabic or Western music they listened to, they had the latest records on vinyl. Men competed for their affection and they turned down many suitors. (Well, my father turned them down, as they usually didn't have the money or social standing he expected for his daughters.) All that was to change, and from then on we would be middle class, without that "upper" prefix that my father, in his best English accent, always added.

Safia was by far the more stoic of the two. She'd gone from being a shepherdess to being the wife of a business tycoon to being a broken man's companion. Perhaps she handled it better than my father or her children for no other reason than her lack of worldly sophistication. Or perhaps she never had the luxury of time for reflection. Her attitude was always simply about surviving another day—another day of cooking for a large family, of hearing stories about my father's philandering, of relatives coming and going and borrowing money. She took part in the mythologizing of Aden just like her husband and older children did, but her participation was often reluctant and punctuated with silences. When she was taken out of Aden, she lost her only safety net, her own three sisters and mother and a society that, despite its colonial moorings, was still tribal and village-like. Her illiteracy didn't stand out in the context of Yemen. With hindsight, I can now understand that Safia's attachment to her mother and sisters was a way of reclaiming her interrupted childhood. She loved to defer to them, to let them make decisions. As soon as they left her house, it was her turn to do the same for her children. She never felt qualified, old or wise enough to call the shots, but she did anyway.

I know that, as much as my siblings and I loved our mother, the difference between our educational levels and her lack of sophistication would become more of an issue as the years went by—years spent in Beirut and Cairo and away from Aden, our paradise lost.

CHAPTER TWO

BEIRUT

Temporary

With his home, business, property and members of his own family—his two brothers, his parents and his oldest daughter, Fathia, who got married in 1966—left behind in Aden, Mohamed had little time for nostalgia or heartbreak. Not right away. It was already late November 1967 and starting a new life in Beirut with nine school-age children would not be easy—especially more than two months into the academic year. As he'd tell us several times, the only thing that kept him from falling to pieces was the impossible list of tasks that needed to be done in a few days. With the family temporarily sheltered in a number of hotel rooms in Raouché, the seaside neighbourhood of Beirut, Mohamed had to find a home big enough for everyone and schools to take in his brood.

The home was easier. After all, a real-estate developer who also happened to know Beirut reasonably well could make his way through the available inventory fast. At the recommendation of a friend, Mohamed and Safia left my sisters Faiza and Farida to look after the children and went to check two interconnected apartments in the then-upscale apartment complex known as the Yacoubian Building. He may have been down and out, but Mohamed would not live below his normal standards. "Too big and expensive," my mother warned him. "I have money," he told her, resenting the suggestion that he could no longer afford the finer things in life, which had become second nature to him over the previous twenty-two years. I don't think he was all that concerned about the cost. To him, this would be a short-term option—the people of Aden wouldn't tolerate the injustice some idealist socialists had inflicted on him, one of society's pillars. In a year or so—"I give it to next June," he wagered optimistically—we'd all be back in Aden. Life would return to normal.

"Sign here," urged the property manager of the Yacoubian Building as my mother tried in vain to dissuade Mohamed from making such a big financial commitment. Sensing that the deal might fall through, the crafty realtor appealed to my father's sense of vanity, which he spotted immediately. He mentioned in a tone half-casual, half-deliberate that the famous Lebanese singer Fahd Ballan and his wife, Egyptian screen goddess Mariam Fakhr Al-Din, called this their home. I don't know if there's a record for how fast a man has signed a lease, but I'm sure Mohamed holds it. A great building with celebrity residents meant that his place in the world remained unchallenged. Revolutionaries and socialists be damned.

One thing he got right. It was a solid building, the kind he would have introduced to Aden had the socialists not taken it over. Revisiting the complex in 2010, almost forty-three years after we had moved in, I was relieved to see it was still standing. It had survived a fifteen-year civil war that destroyed or badly damaged many of the neighbouring properties. Of course, it was rundown and there was less greenery, as more buildings had sprung up around it in the still-beautiful residential area of Caracas. If any artists lived there, they'd be of the struggling and not the glamorous kind. Surprisingly, the elevator with the blue door that we took up and down to the sixth floor still functioned.

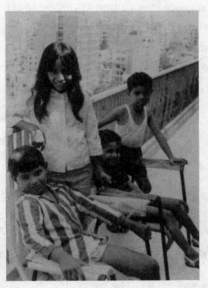

On the balcony of our apartment in the Yacoubian Building in Beirut in 1968, the youngest four children pose for a casual photo. (Left to right: Wahbi, Raja'a, me and Khairy.)

But if finding a home was just a matter of aiming and paying high, choosing schools would be more difficult—even if Mohamed offered to pay full tuition or donate to the school. Knowing how strict school boards tended to be in the central areas of Beirut (imagine a parent calling up Admissions in November to see if they had room for nine children in a day or two), he targeted the suburbs and mountain areas, where the population was less dense and administrators more likely to be charmed by his worldly ways and understanding of local culture. Mohamed loved Lebanese Arabic, which he thought was the classiest version of the language, and loved practising it at home. One school that took students from kindergarten to high school stood out. Literally, as it sat atop the mountainous hamlet of Kafr Shima, about a forty-five-minute drive outside Beirut. Saint Paul's, a Catholic school, admitted all religious faiths and denominations. Mohamed knew that he had to get his children into this school. Having all of them in one place would make the commute easier and the older siblings could look after the younger ones, eliminating the need for him or my mother to go to school whenever a child got sick or into trouble.

We rarely played with other kids in Beirut. In this photo from 1968, my sister Hoda holds me while Hanna and Raja'a smile affectionately at something I said. Wahbi and Khairy look at the camera with their best and goofiest smiles.

I'm not sure what he did or said, but within a week of arriving with nothing but our luggage, we had a home, a school and a new life in Beirut. I'm too young to remember the early days, but as they did about our time in Aden, my family often reminisced about Beirut. It seemed to have everything for a large family of teens and young children to prosper: great beaches, beautiful neighbourhoods, a lively literary, film and theatre culture, excellent shopping. Back then (and it's still the case today), Beirut and Cairo were the two cultural centres of the Arab world. Each boasted a prestigious American university and competed for dominance in music and film. Lebanon's two big divas, Fairouz and Sabah, occupied a special place in the Arab world—the first the height of romanticism and the second of glamour. It was a good time to be a family in Beirut.

My mother didn't see it that way. The Lebanese loved sprinkling their Arabic with either English or French. Her uncultured Yemeni Arabic made her sound like a hick—even in the company of her own husband, who was comfortable with English and passed for a Lebanese when he wanted to. Safia insisted on taking one of her older daughters with her to the market to do the grocery shopping for the first few months until she felt more comfortable in her new world and had memorized the French or English names that locals used for fruits and vegetables.

Mohamed, on the other hand, had to face the possibility that what might have started as a temporary relocation could turn into a long-term situation. His assets in Aden's banks were frozen, so for now his only source of income would have to be the funds he'd stashed away in Britain over the years. One thing about these old colonial types: their faith in England may be annoying and retrograde, but it pays off in some ways. The money in Britain was what he called his last safety net, and even in running his worst-case scenario by Safia in Aden, he never thought he'd have to dip into it.

IF MOHAMED FACED financial ruin, he certainly didn't let his children know or feel its effects. While the days of extravagance in Aden were behind us, we enjoyed a privileged life compared to that of many

Arab families—and even other expatriate Yemeni families. The only sign of retrenching that I can recall was a huge household ledger where my sister Farida was asked to enter every expense that she or my mother incurred. But Mohamed compensated for that with a generous helping of art and entertainment. Lebanese popular culture, like much of the country itself, combined both Western and Arabic influences. As young men and women, my siblings could play a record by Fairouz, to be followed by the latest Beatles single, imported from England. I believe that my family's cultural awareness was formed in Beirut. It was also a scenic place to live—the sea, the mountains, the Roman and Greek ruins. Mohamed took the youngest six children for weekly outings that consisted of either a movie and dinner or just dinner at one of the outdoor restaurants in the more touristy parts of the Raouché neighbourhood. We'd often pose for a photograph or two. We looked like a typical happy family: mother, father and six children, three boys and three girls. But as I look at these same photographs, I wonder now what Mohamed was thinking and how he planned to raise a family as large as his without any real prospect of work or return of income from his property.

The first few months of idyllic living—for the children at least—might have been a fool's paradise anyway. Nearly two decades after the establishment of Israel and the displacement of Palestinians, who became the new underclass in Lebanon and Jordan, the sectarian grudges and skirmishes that divided Lebanon along Druze, Shiite and Christian lines were escalating. "*Ya Allah, ya Allah,*" Mohamed would murmur whenever he saw a news report of an act of violence—a Christian church desecrated or a Muslim business attacked. Our parents advised us children to keep away from Palestinians as troublemakers, to put it mildly. Like many Arabs, they thought nothing of rejecting the Palestinians on a personal basis while recognizing the injustice done to them as a pan-Arab political issue.

Even for a walk downtown and a Sunday matinee, my father dressed in a suit and tie and insisted on a family portrait with his wife and youngest six children.

Still, nothing might come out of the sectarian violence, Mohamed thought, and he continued to insist that our sojourn in Beirut would end soon enough and we'd return to Aden. His favourite phrase when referring to acts of violence in Beirut was the Arabic for "isolated incidents," an idea he must have been clinging to because to believe otherwise was to accept that he had moved his family to the wrong country. The first anniversary of our expulsion came and went and there was still no sign of a change of heart in Aden. If anything, the socialist regime adopted a harder line, aligning itself closer with the Soviet Union and China and pushing Mohamed's dreams of reclaiming his property further from reality.

No one in the family knew for sure what he was up to all day. He had rented a little office in downtown Beirut that he dutifully visited on weekdays. With another expatriate dreamer from Aden, he opened up what was euphemistically known as an export/import business. Translation: anything that came their way. I don't think they made a penny in their first year in business and in all probability lost much of their capital in office rental and, in my father's case, a taxi to and from work every day. (He never took public transport in the Middle East.) Many of the business suits that he'd wear for almost twenty years in Cairo were bought in Beirut at that time. Suits, ties and cufflinks. He wore them even when he took us to a beach. As he didn't have the capital to start a real-estate business and was probably too smart to invest in such an illiquid asset ever again, Mohamed knew he'd always be a small fish from here on.

AS I WAS JUST over three years old when we moved to Beirut, I couldn't join my siblings at Saint Paul's School in Kafr Shima. Instead I stayed home, and Faiza, who had already gone to high school in Aden but didn't wish to go to university, looked after me. My earliest memories of Beirut are of two things that influenced the person I became: music and men. Faiza loved collecting records and would spend all her spare money on Arabic LPs by the likes of Oum Kalthoum, Farid Al-Attrach and Shadia. By the time I was four, I could tell different singers by voice, or at least by the label on the vinyl record. Our daily morning game went something like this: Faiza would play a few seconds from a record and ask me who was singing. When she wanted time for herself, she'd send me back to my mother in the kitchen. "It's your turn," she'd say, and I'd sit in my three-wheel bike watching Safia cook lunch for twelve people.

When both were busy, they'd just park me in front of the TV or give me Arabic celebrity magazines and tell me to look at the pictures. I wasn't five yet when I noticed that I loved looking at a Palmolive ad on TV (and in print) that featured a hairy man, all lathered and grinning because he'd just showered with that brand of soap. Of course I didn't know what that sensation was, but in retrospect it was my earliest homoerotic experience. I was also strangely drawn to the husband, Darrin, on *Bewitched,* which was shown on primetime Lebanese TV. (I didn't realize that two actors played the same part until I saw the show on reruns in Canada decades later.) To me, TV was a gateway into a world of pleasures I couldn't even understand. Whenever I saw Egyptian singer Abdel Halim Hafez on TV, I'd get a strange feeling. He stood out as handsome, romantic and not quite as macho as other actors of his generation.

To Mohamed, however, TV became a barometer for the increasingly volatile situation in Beirut. My brothers and sisters would also report on "incidents" at school or on the school bus, where tensions between older Muslim and Christian students sometimes made the ride home unbearable. You had to know where to sit on the bus— not too close to the Christians so that the Muslim children wouldn't think you a sellout, but not with the Muslim children either, so Christians wouldn't suspect you were shunning them.

My first experience of a bombing dated back to the time I was five, in 1969. A bomb detonated in the parking lot of the Yacoubian Building. Father was at work and I think Faiza must have been out. My mother grabbed me and we ran into the corridor that connected the two apartments, since it had no windows. My memory is a bit fuzzy on the details—who wanted to kill whom— but I do remember Safia asking my sister later in the afternoon to look after me while she stood in the street waiting for her children to come back from school. She wanted to break the news to them. My siblings don't recall having seen policemen or national security agents. They must have come and gone during the day. If I remember correctly, it was business as usual for the rest of the afternoon: lunch, nap, homework. When my father came home, he and Safia retreated to their bedroom and had a long and some-times loud argument. "Where will we go?" my father kept saying. "Anywhere, anywhere but here," Safia said, over and over. I have a feeling my mother's concern for our safety was mixed with her own discomfort about living in Beirut, which never felt like home to her. That argument played repeatedly in the following weeks and months. It was the first time we heard what would become my father's mantra: There was no such thing as security in the Arab world. From here on, he'd say, we had to get used to the fact that security and stability were relative. Apart from a few years in Cairo in the 1970s and Sana'a in the 1980s, Mohamed's words came to pass. If he were alive today, he wouldn't be the least bit surprised by the spreading revolutions or the civil wars in Yemen and Libya. He strongly felt that volatility was the only constant in the Middle East.

We take such things as security and safety for granted in the West, even after 9/11 and the discovery of local terrorist rings. When you send your children to school, you don't worry about them being threatened because of their religious affiliation, and when they come home, it's not often that a parent has to explain what that burnt-out-car smell is all about, or what a bomb sounds like. But that was our experience of Beirut for at least one more year. The Palestinian refugees had in effect set up their own state in the southern parts of Lebanon from which they engaged in a resistance war against Israel. In 1968 Israel retaliated against an attack on one of its planes in Greece by bombing the Beirut airport, including, reports indicate, thirteen civil planes. The balance of power among Maronites, Druze, Shiites and Sunnis—maintained until then for more or less for two decades—was disturbed by the shifting alli-ances within the Muslim communities and the Palestinians. Check-points popped up in the middle of residential streets in Beirut. I just loved all these handsome Lebanese men in uniform who would stop us. Mohamed made a point of carrying his (British) passport with him at all times in case we got stopped on the way back from the movies or dinner.

This was supposed to be a safe haven from Aden?

To make life easier, my mother often dressed her three youngest boys in identical but differently sized shirts. I'm on the far left. This picture, taken at a studio in Beirut in 1969, was always one of my father's favourites.

To make decisions even more difficult, the business in Beirut seemed to be taking off, finally. It even generated some income to relieve Mohamed temporarily from drawing on his savings back in the UK. But was it worth it? What if the next bomb detonated at the movie theatre we frequented, my mother asked him repeatedly, or on our school bus? After asking her to be patient for more than a year, Mohamed came to the same conclusion his wife had. This was a beautiful city, but too unstable to call home.

It was time to leave behind another business. Where to next was still an issue, even though Cairo made immediate sense. It was as familiar to the family as Beirut had become. The only problem was Egypt's state of war with Israel. To my father, moving to a country at war hardly represented a step forward. Jordan, with its own Palestinian refugee population, had an equally troubling recent history. Morocco emerged as a contender, but the fact that we didn't speak French would be a huge problem in finding schools and adjusting to a new life. There was always England, to which we would have been entitled to move as British subjects. But the tax rates for residents would have depleted Mohamed's earnings. Also, by the 1970s, it was too late for my older siblings to start an all-English education. While my father sported a liberal social attitude (for an Arab), he also thought that the England of the Beatles and the sexual revolution would not be appropriate for his children or his own sensibilities, which remained locked in the immediate postwar era.

Cairo it had to be. When his mind was made up, Mohamed asked me to round up my brothers and sisters and bring them to his room. That our father had made *karart hamma* (important decisions) was the news he asked me to deliver. One of the most vivid memories I have of our time in Beirut is of me cycling around the apartment, waking up napping sisters and disrupting my brother Helmi's algebra homework (which he didn't seem to mind at all). All ten children lined up facing our parents, who sat on their separate beds, both dressed in traditional Yemeni clothing. We had been living in Beirut for several years, but at home my mother still wore the *der'a*, a full-length garment usually made of silk or chiffon. It often struck me as too see-through even to wear at home. My father, on the other hand, would abandon his signature suit and tie in favour of the skirt-like *fouta*. Mohamed said something about the difficulty of the decision. My mother held back tears as she grabbed me out of the bike and sat me on her lap. At six, I hardly comprehended what it all meant, but in discussing that evening with my sisters many years later, we all agreed that we were reluctant but relieved to be leaving Beirut. While most Lebanese people were warm and welcoming, a feeling of superiority among them meant that people from such *moutakalef* (backward) Arab countries like Yemen never received equal treatment. The civil war that tore Lebanon apart from 1975 to 1990 is easier to understand when you realize that it's a country where each sect feels more entitled than the next. Beirut's cosmopolitan life was—and still is—seductive, but it's anchored in a feeling of cultural insecurity about its Arabic roots. Nothing describes the country's identity crisis like a T-shirt you can buy in several clothing stores in Beirut nowadays: "Lebanese Identity: Copy and Paste."

Once again, the family would have to say goodbye to a place they called home and friends we had made—albeit this time with more notice. Mohamed waited until the summer vacation in order not to interrupt our education and to allow him time to sell his office furniture. My sisters Farida and Ferial visited the local hairdresser with tears in their eyes. He in turn gave them a copy of a single by an English band whose name I can't remember, but I can still see the numeral 45 printed on its label in large font. We went for one last stroll at the Raouché promenade, or Corniche, and had our pictures taken in a nearby photography shop while Mohamed visited the travel agent to find a flight with thirteen seats, as our grandfather Abdullah was to join the family in Beirut and come with us for a few weeks in Cairo, in part to give Mohamed some support. "Your father is a strong man whom God is testing with this crisis," my grandfather told us when he arrived from Aden. He must have been in his late seventies by then and hardly in good physical condition, but having him around offered some relief to my father, who'd been carrying the family weight on his shoulders for too many years.

There's a reason I smile whenever children run amok on planes. As my grandfather would remind me even when he was in his nineties, I made quite a scene on that plane. It was the first time I had flown since I was three, and it all seemed like exciting fun and games for us younger children. But as Mohamed and Safia sat on that ninety-minute plane ride, they knew they had to start all over again: find a new home and new schools, cope with fresh conflicts and the same old money concerns. So many mouths to feed for one newly unemployed and stressed patriarch. Once again, my parents put on the brave faces they'd perfected in the last few years in Beirut and made a difficult transition look effortless. After all, we all had Cairo to look forward to.

CHAPTER THREE

CAIRO

Arrival

My family's romance with Cairo goes back to the 1960s, but no Arab family could possibly claim that a move to Cairo required much cultural adjustment. As the centre of Egyptian music, film, theatre and publishing—think the London *and* New York of the Middle East—Cairo had always been a familiar place.

In one of those contradictions that even well-informed commentators struggle to explain, Egypt underwent a major intellectual renaissance under the leadership of Nasser, who more or less ran it like a police state. But to my teenage older siblings, Cairo meant sophistication and maturity. Its male movie stars—Roshdi Abaza, Shoukry Sarhan and, of course, Omar Sharif—were drool material for my sisters (and later for me). Records by its singers were never off the many turntables in our Aden and Beirut homes. Although I was too young to recall the last family holiday there in 1966, images and sounds of Cairo from the 1960s are as familiar to me today as they were to my siblings. I seek them out on YouTube and download them on iTunes. To an Arab man of my generation, Egyptian films from that era have the retro and sometimes camp appeal of, say, a

Rock Hudson–Doris Day movie. Gender roles were clearly defined but deliciously subverted. The average plot of an Egyptian movie from the 1950s or '60s revolved around a young couple in love who had to face the old-fashioned and conservative views of their parents or neighbours. Love often triumphed—after six or seven song-and-dance numbers. Cairo always looked clean, inviting, and its buses empty. My earliest memories of Cairo are not all that different from the romantic images I still look for on my computer screen.

After a couple of short-term rentals in the affluent neighbourhoods of Garden City and Zamalek, our new life in Cairo started in 1971 in the more middle-class district of Dokki, an in-between destination that separates Giza and the pyramids from the downtown core of the now world-famous Tahrir Square. Dokki offered a middle place for our new middle-class lives. This time even my father realized that he couldn't throw his money around and house us in the finest apartment building. Safia made sure that he didn't. When it came to signing this lease, she brought along her two oldest daughters. They could talk sense into Mohamed if she couldn't.

Dokki was lively but not too urban. A place where old and new money lived, with plenty of room for the more bohemian types as well. Think of, say, the Annex in Toronto, Islington in London or Greenwich Village in New York. Our new home was a two-level apartment in a 1960s six-storey building overlooking Tahrir Street, the main thoroughfare that runs through Cairo. Directly across from our building we could see the cultural centre for the Soviet Union, a neoclassical white palace that we passed by thousands of times but never ventured into, such was my father's intense dislike of anything socialist or communist. "Propaganda" was his one-word assessment of the superpower's activity across the street as he watched people coming in and out of the building from his favourite lower-level balcony.

My brother Khairy (left) and I pose for a photo on the main-floor balcony of our Dokki apartment in 1971. I still don't know why I'm wearing shorts on what looks like, judging from Khairy's clothes and my own sweater, a cold winter morning.

But if the now-unemployed diehard capitalist preferred to monitor commercial activities, he had no shortage of ventures around him. He could walk up and down Tahrir Street, where restaurants, bookshops, and grocery, clothing and corner stores occupied every storefront. Which he did. As did my mother. Although our stretch of Dokki could hardly be called an intimate neighbourhood, my parents got to know local shop owners well within our first year. Why wouldn't they? When you're shopping for food, clothes and supplies for nine school- and university-age children, you have to spread your wealth and eventually hit most if not all the shops. Saeed, the owner of the news kiosk across the street, made his living off us as he delivered three Arabic newspapers daily and an English one weekly, not to mention the score of magazines to which we subscribed. Every third Friday, Wahbi, Khairy and I—the three youngest children—would sit in the barbershop on the street level of our building and have our hair cut.

My mother bought everything for the household in bulk, especially clothes for the younger children. Twice a year (at the start and end of the school year), she and my father would take the three young male children in a cab to downtown Cairo for our new wardrobe. If Safia liked a shirt, she'd get it in three different sizes and, occasionally, varying colours. I hated that. It made us look like orphans from an old Egyptian film melodrama. While Khairy and Wahbi generally liked whatever my mother selected, I put up fights. Even at that young age, I had a more flamboyant taste. I remember insisting on a pair of burgundy shoes (they looked more like red in Cairo's bright sun) in the winter of 1972, which were incredibly uncomfortable but looked great to my eyes. I hated the wool sweaters Safia particularly liked because she thought Cairo's winters were colder than Aden's (though warmer than Beirut's). It's strange how I have no recollection of ever being cold—or of winter as a different time of year—in all my years in Egypt. Because we didn't have as much money as before, Safia had to ensure that the clothes she bought would last more than one season. She knew where to go to make sure that was the case.

My mother's favourite was a haberdashery shop called Basti, where somehow she spent a small fortune every week on buttons, thread, sewing needles, knitting patterns and a host of other things that strike me now—I who take my shirts to the dry cleaner to replace missing buttons—as artefacts of some ancient art. This was the pre-disposable age of fashion, when you mended your torn shirt instead of buying a new one. The store owner and a young salesman would fuss over my mother, their Big Spender. Whenever she took me with her, I'd get some of the attention. My main memory, however, is not of the merchandise but the fact that the store blasted its air conditioning in the summer—a very unusual practice even in sweltering Cairo. After a few minutes I'd get chilly and start hurrying my mother. She'd swear never to bring me back again. I realize now, of course, that I was intruding on her escape time. In Beirut her worry about not reading or writing Arabic got the better of her, but in Cairo shopkeepers made her feel like the lady of the house she once had been in Aden. They spoke Arabic that was free of English or French idioms, that sounded like all those Egyptian movies and TV dramas she loved to watch—although I was never clear when she found the time to sit in front of the TV and relax. I can't think of Safia without thinking of the kitchen.

After making sure her husband and youngest four children looked their best, my mother sent us out for drinks and ice cream at Kasr el Nil Casino to celebrate Eid, the Muslim feast, in 1972.

I'd rush Safia from Basti in part to take me to my favourite spot—a book and stationery store called Ghomhuria (Republic), down at the heart of the fruit and vegetable market of Suleiman Gohar in Dokki. It sold my favourite comic books, the Adventures of Tintin, in Arabic, and *Mickey,* a weekly Arabic version of the classic Disney characters. The store was still in business when I last visited Cairo in 2010. Like everything else in Dokki, it looks worn out, falling apart. It's that distinct look of faded glory that so many familiar places from my childhood in Cairo now wear—not always well, but with resilience. I didn't have the heart to go in. I tried several times to force myself but felt terrified. This space was once my refuge, and now it looked so alien to me it might as well have been in a country I'd never set foot in. Did I really live here? Was I ever one of the young men I saw hanging out at street corners almost everywhere in the city?

Safia seemed to spend her mornings almost every other day in the market, buying meat, vegetables and lots of bread. I don't understand how we didn't get fat and bloated given how much wheat we ate daily. I don't ever recall being out of bread in Cairo. Safia's typical day would start at six thirty. To ensure hot water for our morning ablutions, she had to manually start the gas-fuelled hot-water heater. We lived in that apartment for ten years and I don't think she ever taught any of us how to light it for fear of burns or gas leaks. Only she could turn it on in the morning and off at night. And because she never left the house for more than a few hours, we never had any worries about having no hot water.

With nine children in school or university by the early 1970s, the family's bathroom routine was a military operation. Two half-bathrooms for bodily functions and one large one for showering and brushing our teeth. No one was allowed more than ten minutes in any of them, and all had to clear up the big bathroom for my father, who would get up before nine every morning and read his favourite Egyptian newspaper, *Al-Ahram,* in the bathroom for almost an hour before taking a shower and going back to his bedroom to pretend to keep up with his business interests. He would type many letters of introduction in English to solicit business from British companies. Almost always he received a standard response to the effect that the company had no plans to expand to Cairo at the moment but that they'd keep his letter for future reference. Mohamed tested my English proficiency as a teenager by having me read his letters and the replies he received. I had a difficult time pronouncing some words: "venture" and "remittance" among them. He'd enunciate with as clear a British accent as he could and correct any hint of American English he detected in me from watching TV shows.

He shared that room with my mother, but they slept in separate beds. Whenever I was sick—and I was a sickly child who missed weeks of school every year—I'd sneak into my mother's bed. It's not the illnesses that I remember but the coded conversations between my parents in the middle of the night.

"*Batkafee?*" (Will it be enough?) Safia would ask Mohamed when he'd tell her how much they could spend on groceries and other household items that week. "*Ya aleem?*" (Who knows?) he'd reply, hinting that it all depended on her spending habits. Perhaps fewer visits to Basti and not as much fruit and vegetables every day? They weren't really bickering but simply trying to ensure that whatever cash my father could get out of his saving accounts in England without depleting them lasted us another year.

He already had to make some compromises and could no longer enrol us in the best schools, house us in the best neighbourhood or clothe us in the best style. Instead, everything had to be second best—a bourgeois lifestyle much more comfortable than the average Egyptian could pull off, but that, to his eyes, ranked much lower than his dreams for his family. In a bizarre sort of way, his tough

decisions forced us into the shabbily genteel, intellectual and cul-
tured segment of Cairo life—a world of books, newspapers, films
and Arab nationalism. Islam was always part of that life, but its
place remained in the background—more cultural expression than
devotional or for that matter activist. Our friends and neighbours
included Muslims and Christians, Egyptians, Syrians, Lebanese,
Greeks, Armenians—and, naturally, other expatriate Yemeni families, since Cairo became the main destination for people from Aden
to wait out the socialist craze that had taken over their homeland. It
proved to be a long wait.

Although the early 1970s—any time after the defeat of Nasser in
the Six Day War of 1967 and his death in 1970—are considered the
beginning of the end of Cairo's renaissance, I recall it as a lovely and
safe place to be a child. The six youngest children—Hoda, Hanna,
Raja'a, Wahbi, Khairy and I—were all enrolled in the same school in
Dokki: Education Home. It was a private Arabic and English school,
one of two that were owned and run back then by a classic Egyptian
matriarch by the name of Nawal Al-Diggoui. She'd drop by every
few weeks unexpectedly and put the fear of God into the score of
teachers and rotating headmasters. She was always over-perfumed
and wore too much makeup. Her imperious attitude marked my
first introduction to Egyptian high society—a world of government officials, judiciary, business tycoons, movie stars and writers
she befriended and whose children were automatically sent to her
schools. You didn't know snobbery and elitism until you met the
Egyptian upper crust. They looked down at Arabs from Yemen or
the Gulf states because they didn't have the same faux French-style
period furniture and gazed at Europe for inspiration in everything
from culture to governance. All of that made my father love them
more and try to ingratiate himself to them. Of course the skeleton
in his closet was my mother, who couldn't spell "France," let alone

find it on a map. She felt more at home with the middle class of Cairo and even its working class.

At the time, my sisters talked of my parents' marriage as the last of the happy unions, but my mother's illiteracy continued to be a source of great pain and embarrassment for Mohamed. She recognized Egyptian money by the sight of each bill, so every time the Egyptian treasury rolled out a new one, she had to stare at it to memorize the imagery and how much it was worth. She'd be shortchanged in the market every now and then, but often hid that fact from my father, whose anxiety about money started to reveal a nasty side in him. About once a year my parents would have a shouting match that almost always had something to do with Safia's mishandling of the household finances. Mohamed would bring up my mother's lack of education almost instantly. "I married beneath me. My mistake." He would say it loudly enough for her to hear even after she had retreated to the kitchen. He would conveniently forget that he made something of his life only after he married her. But although he asked her to economize, he'd berate her if we ran out of, say, his favourite fruit.

I resented my father for putting down my mother, but in all honesty I shared some of his discomfort about Safia's illiteracy, particularly around my schoolmates. Whenever my mother met us outside school to walk us home (and treat us to a fruit drink at a deli in Messaha Square) I'd dread running into friends who might see me or one of my sisters reading signs or price tags for her. My heart would sink when childhood friends showed my mother their monthly report cards. She'd always pretend there was no time or would ask one of us to read her "the highlights" as a way of getting around the issue. Of course, she couldn't always fake her way through almost fifteen years in Cairo. Every now and then a neighbour or family friend would call her on it. Not in a condescending way, but as an incentive for her to take adult literacy classes, which she refused point-blank to do. When I was asked about it, I'd lie and say she was just too lazy to put on her reading glasses.

She didn't care. She relied on her visual memory to get by. She'd only buy what she could see. Ditto for her favourite brand of cigarette, Cleopatra, which of course had the image of the Egyptian queen on all its white packaging. The competing brand, Nefertiti, featured a yellow label and a smaller picture of the queen's head. That's how Safia told them apart. Her main contact with the outside world came from the little black radio in her kitchen, which was set to the Sout Al-Arab (Voice of the Arabs) radio station or the General Program, both part of the government-run media. The latter would play her favourite show: *To Housewives*. Targeted at middle-class Egyptian wives and mothers, the show included everything from health advisories to new recipes to, in the early 1970s, strong and far-from-subliminal messages about socialist values of compassion and helping the less fortunate. My mother's egalitarianism and strong will were reinforced by what she heard on the radio. To my father it was socialist nonsense; to Safia it provided comfort and a sense of belonging—reassurance that her contribution to family life transcended cooking and cleaning and was a political statement and spiritual duty. The Arabic term for "housewife" is *rabat al beit* (house goddess), and she liked the sound of that.

The Cairo of the early 1970s, however, still carried on with the legacy of Nasser's pro-Soviet agenda, which, by necessity, played down—and probably suppressed—the role of religion in Egyptian culture. Our Cairo in the early days was secular. None of us prayed or went to mosques, except on the two high holidays of Eid, and even that was more of a social than a religious obligation for the men in the family. As my sisters approached their twenties, their main pursuit was marriage, and within our first full year in Cairo my second sister, Faiza, received a marriage proposal that she couldn't turn down and that kept the family busy for weeks planning her wedding.

Zaglol—an odd name even in Arabic—was a smart young man from Aden on his way to study in France. His father, an old friend of Mohamed from the heyday of colonial Aden, had made enquiries for an eligible bride with several Yemeni families who had fled for Cairo. Mohamed recommended his second daughter, Faiza, over a cup of tea on the balcony of our Dokki apartment. The groom himself still lived in Aden, taking some intensive French-language training. The idea of being whisked off to France was too romantic for Faiza to pass up, even if marrying someone she didn't know—just as our own mother and father had done twenty-six years before—was considered backward and ran against the modern vibe of 1970s Cairo.

To make her a more attractive choice, my father insisted that Faiza take French lessons at a downtown institute not far from his favourite hangout, the Groppi coffee shop and patio near Opera Square. It was a treat to get invited by our father for ice cream and a soda in the summer or for hot *kunafa* and baklava with custard cream in the winter. My sister told me recently that she and one of her classmates in the French course would drop by for an afternoon tea if my dad was there since he'd pay the bill. I sat on its patio in the spring of 2010 for the first time in almost thirty-five years and imagined what Mohamed's afternoons looked like: coffee, a newspaper, the conversations he'd strike up with English or American tourists who stumbled on his haunt. He needed to practise his English, which he felt was rusting without talking to his British associates in Aden.

By late summer of 1971, when it became official that Zaglol had chosen Faiza for his bride, family attention turned to the wedding.

All weddings are symbolic ceremonies, but this one had an added symbolism and significance for my father. The wedding of his first-born, Fathia, in Aden in 1966, had been a lavish affair—the kind that a business tycoon would throw, both to please his daughter and to assert his place in Aden's turbulent society. This new wedding came after the fall, as it were. It had to restore some of the old glory, even if it meant spending thousands of pounds, which at the time in Egypt would have been an obscene amount of money. As I watch the surprisingly large number of shows on TV now about wedding planners and rich and poor brides, I laugh at some of the impossible tasks my father and older siblings had to undertake in just a few weeks. Booking a banquet hall in a fancy hotel and sending invitations (by hand) was not that different from any wedding in the West today. Of course the boys had to have new suits and the girls new dresses. All of that was to be expected. But Egyptian weddings probably stand out in the entertainment department. The wedding procession—or *zaffa*—is a showcase of wealth and pomp. Nothing but Egypt's top belly dancer, Soheir Zaki, would do for my father. He booked her to lead the couple and guests into the banquet hall and start off the official ceremony with a little hip-swinging. Even at the age of seven, I found watching belly dancing to be hypnotic. I knew it was not a sexual thing, but I admired the art and wildness of it. Years later, as I embraced my gay identity, I would discover that belly dancers were essential parts of Arab camp—Egyptian drag queens impersonate their favourite dancers the way their Western counterparts lip-synch to divas like Barbra Streisand or Madonna.

After the opening belly dance, Soheir posed for pictures with the bride, groom and their families. There's an embarrassing shot of me in the family album looking all flummoxed (in my new three-piece suit) at finding myself in her company. Two Egyptian pop singers whose careers had peaked in the 1960s and were doing the wedding circuit followed. Even Mohamed knew he couldn't afford the top-tier singers. Still, the evening was a success. The marriage less so. Zaglol and Faiza were divorced six years later for irreconcilable differences. My father rarely brought up the fact that they hardly knew each other before they got married, or that he rushed his daughter into the marriage.

I know that my mother found being away from her eldest two daughters—one back in Aden, the other now in France—difficult emotionally. We had to turn down the radio or change the channel whenever we heard songs about absent loved ones, which became a recurrent theme in Egyptian popular music as generations of political dissidents and intellectuals were fleeing Nasser's and then Anwar Sadat's iron-grip rule.

But for us, the younger siblings, having a sister living in France earned us new status in Cairo's Western-obsessed society. Pictures of the couple in the snowbound French countryside were too glamorous not to make the rounds whenever visitors stopped by. Our favourite gifts from France were vinyl albums of British music. My sister Raja'a loved Tom Jones, while Hanna drooled over Engelbert Humperdinck. Two songs from the Tom Jones collection stand out, and to this day bring powerful memories of that lost Cairo: "Love Me Tonight" and "She's a Lady." Of course, the shockingly sexist lyrics of the latter are hard to swallow, but back then I didn't even know what the words meant. I repeated parts of them phonetically. I'd started learning English at the age of five, but it would be another ten years at least before I could sing along to a full Tom Jones record. And to be perfectly honest, I was more interested in the albums because of Jones's sexy poses on the covers. Glittery tight pantsuits and a sexy swagger. Humperdinck always looked like a dork by comparison.

To me those early years in Cairo were simple and innocent. While I wouldn't say I had a frame of reference for those feelings I had for men like Tom Jones, I could at least enjoy fantasizing about singers and movie stars without worrying too much. I was still too young to be expected to act manly or to participate in the machismo of men's lives. I even remember dressing up in women's clothes and putting on a show for my sisters and a visiting aunt with the help of my older brother Khairy, who wore a similar outfit. I added red lipstick to get the look just right. If my sisters' giggles were any indication, our double act was a hit. I, of course, wanted to go back to the wardrobe and create a new outfit. That was in the fall of 1972, to the best of my recollection, and it might as well be the curtain closer on a whole life.

It was the last free display of my latent gay tendencies. The older I got, even while still a child, the less tolerant the family became of my perceived femininity. Whenever I played with a doll or my sisters' nail polish—the smell of which I adored—it would be snatched away from me and I'd be instructed to join my brothers in a game of football. I still don't think of my sisters' and mother's responses as homophobia as we understand it today, but merely their attempt to shield me from bullying in school. In hindsight, their worried looks whenever I indulged in something unusual for a boy of my age were also watchful, and protective.

CHAPTER FOUR

CAIRO

Changes

I n the years following the 1967 Six Day War, Egypt experienced a massive crisis of faith. The war shattered illusions of military might and nationalist pride that for years Nasser had sold his people. The high tone of nationalist Egyptian culture in the 1950s and first years of the 1960s was replaced by a flippant, defeatist, escapist one. Instead of mining Egyptian folklore to glorify their heritage, many composers and writers turned to local art for lascivious notes. Songs about girls taking baths or refusing to drink tea—"I don't drink tea; I only drink Coca-Cola" went one lyric of a popular song—became anthems for middle- and working-class Egyptians who felt betrayed by Nasser. At school we were told not to sing or quote lyrics of such *baladi,* or native songs. They represented a decadence that students of our respectable school were to avoid. But I must admit I wish I was older back then so I could have enjoyed such decadence. What I don't remember, I'm able to glean from Egyptian movies of the period. One of them in particular, *Adrift on the Nile,* summed up the mood in a story about an ethical journalist uncovering an underground network of sex and drugs on a houseboat on the Nile.

(To my utter surprise, in 2006 a multicultural theatre company in Vancouver adapted the novel by Naguib Mahfouz on which the film was based.)

We had this picture taken at a photography studio on Tahrir Street in Cairo to celebrate Wahbi's birthday in 1972. Khairy (left) and I are dressed in vests, the latest fashion, although mine, in shades of brown, is clearly oversized.

My consciousness as a growing boy in Cairo started with another war against Israel, the war beginning on October 6, 1973, known by Israelis as the Yom Kippur War. No matter how secular you were and how many Jewish families you knew, if you lived in the Egypt of the 1970s, Israel was the enemy. At school, Israelis were portrayed as unlawful occupiers of Palestinian land and killers of children. Our school held several fundraisers and charity concerts for Palestinian refugees during which footage of displaced children and women were shown. Most Arabic families publically used the word "Jewish" as a synonym for someone who exploited or threatened innocent victims. It took years of cultural readjustment and conscious effort to disassociate the two in my mind. The early days of the short-lived war, when it looked like Sadat's army had the upper hand, shocked many Egyptians out of their complacency and revived the fortunes of the country's military forces, which explains their continued place in the country's politics.

To me the war at first just meant a few days off school. Even though it was fought in the Sinai desert, Cairo was under watch for possible air raids. For my father, who was still largely unemployed and plotting his "comeback," the war meant a further delay of his business plans. But it was a worthy sacrifice. "Even the date of October 6 has a ring to it," he'd tell his brother Hussein, who was visiting from Aden at the time. The new military anthems, hastily released to win the PR war, used the date in what you might call now a branding exercise. "The sixth of October reunited us as a nation—an Arab nation" were the words we were forced to sing for months afterwards during morning assemblies. And as soon as injured soldiers were shipped to Cairo hospitals, the school arranged bus trips for the students to pay tribute to the "heroes." My mother intensely disliked these new trips to faraway military hospitals, in part because you could never show up empty-handed and she had to buy us boxes of chocolates to give the soldiers.

Money was getting tight just as Safia's children were growing up and demanding more. The household expenses gobbled up all our income, which now consisted only of the interest—and occasionally part of the principal—of my father's savings in the UK. When the exchange rate of the English pound went down, so did our disposable income. On weeks with exchange-money surplus, my parents took the youngest four children to the cinema on Thursday nights. Every other month, Mohamed would drag us to the more expensive live theatre to watch popular Egyptian comedies. Performances always started as late as 10 p.m. and would last until 1 or 2 a.m., by which time I would have fallen asleep in my mother's lap.

The inflation that hit the West after the 1973 war also hit Egypt and our family's finances. Until then, if you were poor in Egypt you somehow still managed to eat a full meal and have a roof over your head. By 1974 even such basics proved more than many Egyptians could afford. I cringe when I think that the cleaning maids my parents hired at the time got paid ten to twenty Egyptian pounds a month. No wonder they occasionally stole food from the kitchen or small household items—which infuriated my mother, who felt the pinch herself. Our maid for many years, Enayat, came from the working-class district of Shoubra and always showed up for work late because of the crowded buses and traffic congestion. She was only in her forties but had severe back and neck pains and was a widowed mother of, if I remember correctly, two teenage children. She always had bruises on her arms or legs or came in with her traditional Egyptian clothing all covered in dirt, as she kept tripping and falling when running to catch the overcrowded bus. She ate the leftovers from our lunches and dinners and wrapped up what she didn't get through in a white scarf to give to her children. Even back then, Enayat would recall the better days of the 1960s and complain about this new, harsher way of life in Cairo. By no means am I suggesting that there was a social cohesiveness in Egyptian society before then, but in the years after the 1973 war the country divided along economic lines: the ultra rich, the struggling middle classes and the impoverished poor.

CHANGE. AGAIN. THIS TIME the pace was slower but the effect just as long-lasting. Stories of break-ins, muggings and violent crimes became part of our lives. They usually took place in more impoverished parts of town or very late at night, but like all middle-class families we had to watch our backs. We could sense the anger of some Egyptians and, as the civil war in Lebanon was starting in 1975, also feel it in the waves of Palestinian and Lebanese refugees. Nasser's agenda of a secular pan-Arabism had broken apart only four years after his death.

By 1976, my oldest brother, Helmi, was the first to bring some of these hardened attitudes inside the family home. A handsome, secular law student at Cairo University, Helmi fell under the spell of rebellious Egyptian middle-class men his age who discovered that neither socialism nor Sadat's new free-trade philosophy and nascent pro-capitalism would improve lives. Islam, until then relegated to the sides of the political landscape, emerged as an alternative. For many years Sadat's mantra went something like this: No politics in religion and no religion in politics. It outraged young Egyptians and the Muslim groups, which until then had been relatively quiet. I wish I could say the ideological shift in Helmi was gradual, or that our parents had time to wean him off it. The truth is that one summer day in 1976, he woke up to tear down the posters of movie stars in his room (including a gorgeous one of Clint Eastwood circa 1973 that I secretly adored), rearranged his bedroom to make space for a prayer mat that faced Mecca, and just like that found Islam.

Even though Helmi's notion of a return to Islam would be called moderate by today's standards of militarized hard-liners, my father—ever the secularist—became deeply concerned about this conversion. For one thing, it meant that Helmi was mixing with young men beneath his social status, and for another, it became a case of a son trying to control family destiny while the father was still alive and well. Islam undercut Mohamed's authority as a patriarch. He did try to change Helmi's new direction. He'd often challenge him on his notion of Allah as a furious, punitive force. To my father, Islam was more about ethics, compassion and charity. It had nothing to do with banning belly dancers or censorship of art and culture. And it certainly should not interfere with how money was made or interest rates were determined. "Why would God throw me in hell," he argued with Helmi, who would reply, "Because you don't pray five times a day or fast at Ramadan." Mohamed would counter by saying that he went about his business and raised eleven children, and raised them well. That to him was more important than praying or fasting.

But if Helmi's change of direction was fought on a symbolic and ideological level with his father, it was the beginning of an oppressive time for my sisters from which they have not yet recovered—and which long ago eroded their will to resist.

MY FIVE REMAINING SISTERS in Cairo—Farida, Ferial, Hoda, Hanna, Raja'a—were very much integrated into Egyptian society. That meant coming and going as they pleased, wearing whatever they thought was fashionable and appropriate, including miniskirts, and applying as much or as little makeup as the occasion demanded. I loved that about my sisters and my parents back then. The family pictures of the time stand as testaments to the last great wave of Arab social liberalism and secularism.

For young women like my sisters in the Cairo of the early 1970s, the idea of wearing a hijab was unthinkable. To young Egyptians, it symbolized poor and uncultured country folks—the kind who were to serve as maids and not as fashion models. (The hijab's association with oppression of women is a newer, Western phenomenon.) Egypt's large cities—Cairo and Alexandria—had gone through a great period of modernization starting in the 1920s, during which women adopted Western dress and abandoned traditional garb. That came to an end in the late 1970s and throughout the 1980s.

Nothing symbolized the freedom we had as a family as much as our annual summer vacations in Alexandria and the bikini-shopping ritual beforehand in downtown Cairo, which brought out the fashionista in me, even at the tender age of ten or eleven. I looked forward to it every summer and spent the weeks before going through women's magazines and cutting out my favourite designs. I have absolutely no recollection of the men in the family raising any objections, although I suspect that my parents were secretly concerned about indulging this feminine side. Egyptian cinema featured several distressing stereotypes of the effete (never explicitly described as gay) fashion designer, florist or dance instructor. By the end of the movie these figures often got humiliated by the macho leading man. I wonder if my mother thought I was headed in that direction—which I certainly was.

My father dressed in a suit even for a day at the beach with his children. This photo shows our last family trip to Alexandria, Egypt, in 1976. A mere year or two later, the thought of my sisters wearing bikinis was unacceptable.

"The colour of this brown two-piece makes you look darker," I'd tell my sister Raja'a as she went through the swimwear selection in a crowded shop near Talat Harb Street in downtown Cairo. She picked a lime-green bikini instead. "I love this one so much I want to wear it myself," I blurted out to Ferial, clinching her choice of a black-and-white striped swimsuit. When we eventually got to the beach, Mohamed—in his summer suit and tie—and Safia would listen to the radio or talk to other Egyptian families nearby while all the children got into the water. None of us were swimmers as such, but the point was to leave Cairo for two weeks at the hottest time of the year.

I believe that our last trip was in 1976. By the following year, Helmi's embrace of Islam was getting stricter, and his constant berating of our sisters for their love of "risqué" clothes or excessive makeup was drowning out my father's constant praise. His daughters were *helween* (beautiful), he'd tell them. When Mohamed was really feeling generous and Safia was within earshot, he'd add, "Just like your mother." The old flirt may have lost his wealth but not his way with women. His women, at least. It must have been hard on him to realize that all the women he prided himself on catching back in Aden were probably into him for the money. In Cairo, while still comfortable, he was just a middle-aged man with eleven children.

EVEN AS A CHILD I did not escape Helmi's transformation. I looked up to him, but he'd ignore me until I joined him in prayer, which even at thirteen or so I didn't feel like doing. I didn't understand the point of being religious; I associated it with old people. During the holy month of Ramadan, I'd hear no end of it if I didn't fast or if I spent the day playing instead of reading the Quran. "Leave him alone—he's still a baby," my mother told Helmi repeatedly. "He's as big as a horse," Helmi would answer back. I was already nostalgic for the days when we were an all-secular household. My immediately older brother, Khairy, was more amenable to this new form of religious observance, and soon enough he was telling me and my other brother, Wahbi, off for not praying or going to the mosque on Fridays with him and Helmi. Wahbi and I cared more about music and film and were in the habit of sneaking out to movie theatres on Fridays (our day off from school) to watch the latest Arabic or foreign releases. Going to a mosque seemed like a waste of a weekend. Who needed to spend his free day listening to an angry imam and watching scores of men nodding in agreement?

My sisters Raja'a (right) and Ferial and I pose with our first-born niece, Rasha, in 1978. Note my afro—I was also wearing bell-bottomed jeans and high heels. I'd started listening to American disco music by then and liked the fashion that accompanied it.

Similarly, my sisters did their best to ignore Helmi's criticism (and later Khairy's) and continue with their regular beauty and fashion routine. But there was only so much you could do before you started self-censoring—self doubting is more like it—and taking safer options. The skirts got longer, the makeup lighter. Dyeing their hair was for special occasions. A new reality set in.

My sister Farida, Child Number Three in the family and the next in line to get married, had a glamorous career and looks to match. Statuesque, even-tempered, with a good secretarial training from the American University in Cairo's School of Continuing Education, Farida found a job in 1974 as a secretary at the Liberian embassy in Cairo. Her salary of three hundred US dollars a month would have been considered very high in Cairo back in the 1970s, and probably by many Egyptians today. More importantly, the job opened up the world of the international diplomatic community to her, which came with parties, receptions and a string of gentlemen admirers. I'd sit up in the early evenings during the school year and watch her apply her makeup or get dressed in the room she shared with two of my other sisters. It didn't take me long to insist that she come to school on parent-teacher nights. My mother must have known I was afraid it would be discovered that she was illiterate, and she often came up with an excuse not to go and asked Farida to fill in for her.

There were months when Farida's take-home pay exceeded what my dad earned from his savings. She was expected to cover household expenses, which made my mother angry. Safia wanted her husband to stop messing about and get some work—not live off his own daughter. My parents started to argue more frequently and passionately about money. We lived in fear of yet another fight. My mother may have been uneducated, but she never backed down from arguing with Mohamed when it came to providing for her children. When my grandparents would visit—especially my father's parents—they repeatedly asked her not to butt heads with their son, as he was the man of the house. "You should know better," they told her. When my grandmother was feeling particularly vindictive, she'd remind Safia that Mohamed could have married a more beautiful and lighter-skinned girl. She'd add that it was not too late for him to seek a less nagging wife. My father would have been fifty-two or fifty-three, which I guess was not too old for a second marriage, but the idea of leaving the mother of his children only came up during fights. All this took place in front of us children. It was a lesson not in family relations but in money management. Even before I fully apprehended the meaning of my sexuality, I made up my mind not to have more than one or two children so I could afford to raise them. When I told my brother Wahbi this before we went to the movies, he laughed and told me not to be so melodramatic.

ONCE MOHAMED REALIZED that our survival depended on the income of one of his daughters, he finally abandoned his pride and in 1978 sought employment in Saudi Arabia. The Gulf countries had a severe labour shortage and recruited heavily from countries with surplus populations like Egypt or Lebanon, where the civil war was into its third year by then. He found a job as an independent contract and business negotiator for a number of well-to-do Saudi families of Yemeni extraction, including the powerful dynasty of bin Laden—a name that was associated with obscene wealth long before it became a symbol of Islamic terrorism. Of course, our connection with the bin Ladens went back to the early decades of the twentieth century, as my mother was born and raised in their native Hadhramaut.

Because of visa regulations, only my father as a businessman could enter and work in Saudi Arabia in the 1970s. That meant leaving his family behind for the first time since the late 1940s, when he sailed from Aden to study in England. Mohamed talked often about the hardship of working in Saudi Arabia—living alone, the egotism and capriciousness of the local businessmen and, particularly for the secular philanderer from Aden, the kind of religious intolerance he observed in the country. He'd often tell us about the "barbaric" custom of the religious observance police, the *mutaween,* who rounded up people during prayer time and herded them into mosques. But a decade of no serious work or income meant having to put his personal beliefs aside and adopt, in appearance at least, a kind of religious piety that would keep his business associates happy.

Back in Cairo, Helmi's grip on his sisters only strengthened with our father's frequent absences. Ironically and appropriately enough, Helmi struggled to finish law school at Cairo University even when his supposed new religiosity freed up the time he had spent, say, watching TV or hanging out with his family at the Ahli Club, the sports and social club we were members of in the Gezira part of Cairo. The more courses he failed, the more observant he became. "Maybe he should pick up a textbook instead of the Quran," my mother would tell her neighbour, the widowed wife of an army captain, during one of their regular lunchtime chats.

Our neighbour also had a son who was suddenly interested in Islam after years of secular living and education. The two mothers knew that such transitions didn't bode well for the families involved or the country itself. I listened in on many of their conversations over the year, as I continued to seek shelter in the kitchen whenever and for however long I could. Our kitchen and the neighbour's backed on to each other, with a little porch and the garbage chute separating the two apartments.

It strikes me as odd that the women in our circles of Cairo were the ones who noted and expressed concerns about the men's—usually young men's—new directions when the most visible sign of such change in society came from women lower down the social ladder. I was floored the first time I saw a young middle-class Egyptian woman wearing the hijab at school. Education Home was a co-ed institution that encouraged equality between the sexes, so it came as a shock to the bourgeois system to have a mid-term English replacement teacher by the name of Miss Afaf assigned to our class. Today you'd be hard pressed to find a female schoolteacher in Cairo who was not wearing the hijab, but back in 1977, in my first year of secondary school, Miss Afaf caused a sensation. We'd heard of some young women donning the hijab and even saw some of them on TV as part of a current-affairs story about the lives of young Egyptians. But to have someone like *her* in our school was the subject of much debate among the different cohorts. She was an excellent teacher and very gentle, but we just couldn't get past her headwear.

Neither could some parents. It seemed that Miss Afaf did not stick to teaching English grammar and vocabulary but set herself the goal of persuading many of the young women in class—thirteen and fourteen years old on average—to cover up their own hair and follow the rules of Islam, since it was the right and only path. Her first convert was the most beautiful girl in my class: Fadwa, a petite blond Libyan-Italian stunner, who covered her hair for a few days before her mother came charging in and asked the school headmistress to keep Miss Afaf away from her child. Other parents congregated outside the school and discussed this new phenomenon. My mother didn't get involved in the discussions, but even she didn't like having a teacher with a hijab in school. None of this had much to do with an anti-Islam or a pro-secularity sentiment and everything to do with social hierarchy and prejudice. Mothers considered women like Miss Afaf too far down the social ladder to teach at a private school like ours. Many of the parents probably resented having to pay hefty tuition fees for the kind of teacher that staffed government schools.

Miss Afaf didn't return to school the next academic year. But that's not to say she was an isolated incident. In Cairo at the time, the line between class and religion was drawn—the more affluent you were, the less religious, and the same was true in reverse. Cairo was fighting a losing battle against a rising tide of politicized Islam under the banner of the regrouped Muslim Brotherhood. The reasons for this new surge are both political and economic. After over two decades of suppression by Nasser, his successor, Anwar Sadat, released many of the Brotherhood's organizers from jail—a political gesture that would cost him his own life when he was assassinated in 1981 by a convert to the group. Economically, Sadat's open-market policies and pro-Western-style capitalism—symbolized by the reopening of the Suez Canal as a trading post in 1975—created huge gaps between the haves and have-littles. Hundreds of thousands of Egyptian workers left the country to seek employment in Saudi Arabia, Iraq or other oil-rich Gulf states while the inner circle of Sadat—and later Mubarak—would reap the rewards of economic reforms. For the first time since the 1952 revolution, average Egyptians couldn't count on the quasi-socialist state to help them survive. In fact, with increased police brutality and widespread corruption among government workers, the state became the enemy of the people. I dismiss as incomplete analyses of the rise of fundamentalism and, by association, terrorism that do not trace the roots of both to that transitional moment in Egyptian history. And because Egypt exerted a huge cultural and moral influence on other Arab countries, the shift towards a more politicized and economics-driven notion of Islam quickly spread to other parts of the region.

Even as an expatriate Yemeni family in Cairo, we began to feel the tensions in the air—literally so. The Friday prayers were—and still are—the most direct way of gauging the political mood in a city like Cairo. This might explain why most of the more turbulent events of the recent Egyptian revolution took place on Fridays, including, for example, the storming of the Israeli embassy in September 2011. The call to prayer would often be followed with a call to action. Since local mosques started to use amplification to reach the increasing number of people who prayed on makeshift carpets on the streets, we couldn't help but hear the Friday *khoutba* (sermon) from our Dokki apartment. Gone were the speeches about the history of Islam or the interpretation of domestic or economic laws. The new imams were virulent, waging a war on what they saw as decadence and corruption in Egypt's government and the wider society. Their favourite target was Sadat himself; their second was what they perceived as the loosening of moral codes in Egyptian society. They offered a long list that included, among other topics, women going out alone and working late into the night, and the pernicious influence of Egyptian films and music—once a source of national pride—on the morals of young Muslims. My sister Hoda and I sat on our balcony and listened to these direct attacks on the arts and artists with great interest but greater apprehension. I can't say that we comprehended the meaning of all these diatribes or that we didn't find the colourful language and lyric-quoting to be funny. I mean, there's something inherently comic about an old imam quoting at length from folkloric Egyptian music—songs about bathtubs calling for young ladies to wash themselves or others that used the word "prophet" or "God" in the title. Lyrics that sounded perfectly normal in a pop song acquired a surreal meaning when repeated by a religious figure.

I hated Fridays, at least until after the noon prayers wrapped up. My idea of happiness and my cultural inspirations were derived from Arabic music and cinema at first, and then American and British influences. The constant bashing of everything I liked made me feel I could never belong in this world. Just a couple of years before, none of my family would have thought it odd if one of my sisters' male colleagues called one of them on the phone—for business or just a friendly chat. Now the friends had to play a little game where they got their own sisters to dial and ask for one of my female siblings before handing over the phone to their brother. It varied from family to family, but with the new brand of Islam came a regressive segregation of the sexes.

It started to become clear that the secular Egypt we relocated to in the beginning of the decade was under threat by the end of it—seven years that changed a city, a nation and possibly the world we live in now, since so many of the 9/11 hijackers came out of the same culture that festered in Egypt in that decade. As my father returned for family visits, you could see the look of concern on his face. With Beirut in the midst of a full-fledged civil war by then, options were running out for finding a new home for his nine unmarried children—and for my sister Faiza, whose marriage to Zaglol came to an unhappy end as well.

CHAPTER FIVE

CAIRO

Radical

Ideological shifts in Cairo's society coincided with personal changes and realizations. I knew I was different from my brothers and friends at school in that I was not interested in girls, sexually or romantically—even though I was popular with my female classmates, the earliest example in my life of "fag hags" that I can remember. There's no such thing as sexual education in the Arab world, so I had no concept of homosexuality or even much of an awareness of such rites of passage as reaching puberty. We may have been a secular family, but we didn't talk freely about sex. I always masturbated about men and was turned on by handsome Egyptian movie stars like Hussein Fahmi, who had a very European look, with fair hair and green eyes; or, my favourite, Mahmoud Yassin, who was more traditionally Egyptian looking—dark olive skin, dark brown eyes and thick black hair. I bonded with my sisters over our adoration of these two leading men of Egyptian cinema in the 1970s. To me they represented ideals of masculinity and beauty and were never far from my dirty little mind as a young boy. I smuggled movie magazines into the bathroom and kissed their pictures.

There was no one I could talk to or ask for guidance. When, in the summer of 1977, one of my masturbatory sessions ended with an ejaculation, I seriously thought I was being punished by God for my sins. I'd never heard of ejaculation or seen semen and, to use a more modern expression, freaked out. This, I told myself, was a sign, a punishment for my anti-religious views and for refusing to go to the mosque on Fridays. I had to renounce all carnal thoughts and desires and look for something in Helmi's bookshelves that might explain what had just happened. Those bookshelves were once home to English classics and Arabic translations of great world literature—this was where at twelve I first read an abridged version of Charles Dickens's *A Tale of Two Cities* and, in Arabic translations, was introduced to great nineteenth-century Russian writers like Dostoevsky and Tolstoy, who came to prominence in Egypt during Nasser's socialist years. Now the shelves were filled with interpretations of Islam by mullahs I'd never heard of and a stream of books about signs of the Apocalypse—a sub-genre of Islamic literature that has, as I saw on a visit to Cairo more than thirty years later, clearly remained popular.

There I found it, in one of the books: homosexuality, or in Arabic *shozoz* (aberration). There was a passage about how it made God angry and that He preferred that men copulate with stones before they did it with each other. A story about Lot and Sodom followed, as did suggestions for how to overcome homosexuality and punishments for those who embraced it. Celibacy, constant prayer and reading of the Quran constituted remedies; stoning and flogging deterrents. Not much by way of options for the naive thirteen-year-old that I was. I tried the prayer and Quran-reading combo for a few weeks, part out of fear and part hoping that my older sisters might offer me some guidance in sexual matters. I quickly abandoned that hope when, by chance, the subject of homosexuality was alluded to during a casual conversation between Faiza and one of the many house guests from Aden who for some reason always landed in our Cairo apartment. I don't remember the context of the conversation, but it ended with my sister telling her guest that should their mutual friend ever brag about her life or show off in her annoying way, they should remind her that her husband was a scumbag who liked to bugger young boys—the lowest of the low. The image of the older man who preyed on boys was by far the most prevalent representation of homosexuality in contemporary Arab culture, followed closely by the effete decorator or florist that I mentioned earlier. Although that didn't necessarily put me off homosexuality, it made talking openly about it to anybody in my family next to impossible. I stuck it out with religion for a few weeks. It didn't make me feel any better or answer my questions about sexuality—but it was something.

Until Sobhi came into the picture later the same year.

Sobhi was the Man Friday in the apartment building where we lived. A working-class Egyptian about twenty-one or -two at the time and every bit the sex symbol for me. He lifted weights and was into wrestling. To me that was manliness. He always looked after me and tousled my hair on my way to and from school—sometimes making sarcastic remarks about being the spoiled youngest child and sometimes just smirking. One day in September 1977, Sobhi and I were sharing an elevator ride when he pushed the Stop button between floors. He unzipped his trousers and starting playing with his penis and encouraged me to take out mine. It was my first sexual experience and, frankly, I was confused, because I assumed that Sobhi was the kind of straight guy who beat up effeminate men on the street. As he asked me to put my hands around his penis, we heard other tenants shouting to know if everything was okay with the elevator. Sobhi pushed the Go button and we went up one floor and took the stairs to the level between the penthouse and the roof, where rarely anybody dropped by. He jerked off, explaining how much fun it was, and left it at that.

So it turned out that ejaculation was a natural bodily function and masturbation not my own private sin. I wasn't being punished by Allah after all. "Everybody does it," Sobhi assured me. I never told Sobhi this, and I don't even know if he's still alive, but he changed my life in that one afternoon encounter. Not only did I feel somehow liberated from the shackles of religious ignorance, but if manly men like him liked same-sex encounters, then I shouldn't complicate my life. I was ecstatic. I'd had a sexual encounter that my friends would envy me for—if Sobhi had been a girl. I still trace the roots of my gay identity, in a social and political sense, to that day.

SOBHI SHOULD HAVE BEEN in the army, but as the only son and main provider in his family he was probably exempt from military service. As the Egyptian uprising of 2011 showed, the military is the largest public institution in that country during peacetime—so you can imagine its might and influence in 1977, when Egypt was still in a state of war with Israel over occupied territories in Sinai and around the Red Sea.

By November 1977, however, President Anwar Sadat made a remarkable visit to Israel to seek a peaceful resolution to the differences between the two countries. For every adult Arab, this turned into a historic and ambivalent moment. It symbolized hope, betrayal, weakness, strength, servitude to the American imperial agenda and independence from it. We all sat in front of the TV watching the president's Egypt Air plane landing on Israeli soil. The only comparable history-making event in North America would be the moon landing in 1969 or the election of Barack Obama in

2008. Naturally, skepticism took over Helmi, who accused Sadat of betraying the Arab and Muslim cause, whatever that might be. Our father and, to our surprise, mother were far more optimistic and supportive. By then, Safia had seen one too many Egyptian families bid farewell to sons entering the army—some of whom never made it back alive after the 1973 war.

The state-controlled media allowed little room for debate and covered Sadat's visit as a great and brave step forward for all Egyptians. Patriotic songs that chanted death to the Zionists instantly disappeared from the airwaves and were replaced by hastily composed paeans to the bravery of Sadat and the eternal appeal of peace. Such simple framing of the issue did not sit well with diehard Islamists and old Nasserites, who felt that the country's place as the centre of religious scholarship and its pan-Arab national pride were eroded by this visit, and by the Camp David peace treaties that followed it.

The socialist republic of South Yemen joined a small group of Arab countries (Libya and Syria, among others) to cut off diplomatic relations with Egypt for its newly negotiated peace with Israel. As natives of Aden, South Yemen's capital, living in Cairo, we felt the brunt of our home country's stance. For the first time ever in Cairo, we felt different, slightly ostracized by Egyptian society. If we could help it, my father told us, we should try not to reveal where we came from. As permanent residents we couldn't be expelled from Egypt— and technically, we held North Yemeni passports, so on the level of paperwork we were safe. But many families we knew from Aden who were visiting or studying in Egypt's various universities were on the receiving end of what my father often called the Arab world's destiny of chaos and instability. Many of these families got kicked out of Egypt with just a few days' notice. Stories of students being rounded up and held in detention centres before being put on planes spread in the Yemeni community in Cairo. Our upper-floor balcony, which overlooked a side street, became a dumping ground for friends from Aden who had no choice but to leave their heavier baggage behind and travel as light as possible. Who knew where they'd end up? Almost all were deported directly to Aden, while others chose Syria to complete their education. None of them reclaimed their bags, which sat on the balcony as mementos of the cruelty of Arab regimes towards one another. Before too long, my mother asked us to open the bags, take what we wanted and throw away the rest. It felt like a violation of privacy—I remember seeing a condom packet for the first time, not knowing what it was before it was snatched from my hands.

At school, the political differences were starting to make morning assemblies and recess very difficult. The brainwashing of Egyptian youth didn't take long, and anyone who disagreed with the president's choices—or came from a country that did—represented a danger. In an attempt to make my life easier, I asked to read a piece—in English—at assembly that praised Sadat for "seizing the opportunity of peace." I remember that phrase very well, because Farida rewrote most of the text for me and helped me with the pronunciation of bigger words. It was, admittedly, a sycophantic piece of writing, but it bought me some reprieve from the bullies and favour with the teachers.

THERE WAS ONE BRIGHT SIDE to the normalization of relations between Egypt and Israel: I discovered Barbra Streisand, who remains my favourite artist of all time. I vaguely remember my sisters going to see *Funny Girl* in Beirut in 1969 and then playing the song "People" on vinyl. As a singer who was so identifiably Jewish and perceived as pro-Israeli, she was banned from Egyptian airwaves for much of the 1960s and '70s. Omar Sharif, her co-star in *Funny Girl*, also came under special watch, although his pre-Hollywood Arabic films aired on Egyptian TV all the time. By early 1978 the ban was lifted and local distributors released Streisand's movies to Egyptian cinemas for the first time. My introduction to her was *A Star Is Born,* which Ferial took me to see in the winter of that year.

I still don't understand what happened to me that afternoon in Cinema Kasr el Nil in downtown Cairo. I've never been so hypnotized by a singer before. I was beginning to discover Western music—a bit of ABBA, a little Tina Charles and a lot of Olivia Newton-John—but Streisand represented a different world of sexual and social freedom. I was probably more attracted to her co-star, Kris Kristofferson, but his music, in the film at least, sounded dreadful to me. The theme song from *A Star Is Born,* "Evergreen," was like a siren song for a gay Muslim boy in Cairo at the time. I quickly caught up with *Funny Girl* and *Funny Lady* in other cinemas later that year. Because of their period settings, I was somewhat underwhelmed by them. But when I saw *What's Up, Doc?* shortly thereafter, I was hooked again. I was thrilled when a TV show of Western music, *The World Sings,* put cuts from *A Star Is Born* on rotation. I didn't always understand the lyrics and had to rely on the subtitles, but it didn't matter. We had one of those seventeen-inch black-and-white TV sets with a built-in cassette recorder in my sisters' room, so I made decent copies of the songs and played them before going to school and as soon as I got back.

Shortly after that I settled in on two Western divas who represented different images and aspirations for me: Newton-John for her pre-*Grease* sweetness, and Streisand for representing a sexual energy I couldn't understand. I had no idea about her gay following at the time and wouldn't have understood the word "camp" even if you charted its history and made me memorize it. Naturally, this new obsession with Western singers didn't sit well with Helmi, who often criticized the music as lacking the depth and artistry of Arabic compositions. I ignored him. It was harder, however, to ignore my father, who seemed genuinely concerned about my fascination with Streisand in particular. To this day I still don't understand his aversion to her. It couldn't be her Jewishness, because I strongly believe that had no bearing on him, as he grew up in an Aden that was racially and ethnically mixed. He was also quite Westernized in his thinking and valued the English language and culture, whether in its British or American guises. My guess is that he sensed my nascent homosexuality and was both disapproving as a parent and worried about the trouble that awaited me because of it in the Arab world. He'd constantly remark on the beauty of Newton-John to see if he got a reaction from me. He could never remember her full name—just Olivia. By that time he was working in Saudi Arabia more and was losing contact with his children. As I was the youngest, and in his opinion most vulnerable, my discovery of Western music and Streisand in particular spelled trouble.

Early in 1979, and much to my delight, *A Star Is Born* was shown on Egyptian state TV as the feature film in a Saturday-night program called *Cinema Club*. It was a late show that started after 10 p.m. on a school night. Almost all my brothers and sisters were in bed. Only Ferial, my father and I stayed up to watch it. It was an uncomfortable experience, especially given some of the sex scenes in the movie that were not cut by the censor, and my father, a fan of 1940s Hollywood musicals, hated the rock soundtrack. I kept falling asleep and tried my best to stay awake by rushing to the bathroom and throwing cold water on my face every fifteen to twenty minutes. I'm not sure which Mohamed watched more, me or the screen. Either way, we both stayed up until the end credits. He almost got up to turn off the TV during the finale, a gorgeous song called "Watch Closely Now," in which the camera zoomed in on Barbra, with her big afro hair and man's suit. But he knew that would break my heart and went back to his seat. When he switched off the TV, he looked at me and said, *"Allah yerdi alek"* (May God keep you content). I don't think my fourteen-year-old brain could process what that meant. What had God got to do with anything? We'd just watched a great modern musical with a fantastic leading lady. Ferial told me to forget about it and go to bed.

IN RETROSPECT, THAT EVENING marked the beginning of a drift between my father and me that would last until just before his death in 1995. Even if he didn't detect the sexuality, he probably sensed the impending rebellion. The Middle East was not the safest place to be different. As he spent more and more time in Saudi Arabia, the old liberal womanizer was fading and the fifty-something conservative parent taking over.

With my father and brother both leaning towards conservative values, I sought family refuge in my mother, whose lack of sophistication about bigger life directions became comforting to me. But even she was probably concerned that as a growing boy of fourteen I was spending so much time in the kitchen, a decidedly female space in the Arab household. Still, Safia was a devoted mother who lived to make her children happy. My greatest happiness was to get extra allowance money and buy more Western music and posters and bring home more magazines that featured lyrics to hit songs so I could sing along. My sisters certainly encouraged me. Perhaps they saw my new passions as a counterbalance to the hardened lines of the men in the family. My weekly treat was to go shopping with any of my sisters in downtown Cairo's high-end Shawarbi Street. This was where imported fashions went on sale and where my favourite record shop sold bootleg cassettes of hit American and British music. Window-shopping alone was an education, as I'd make note of artists and album titles—some of which I'd look up in an English-Arabic dictionary—and check with like-minded friends in school to see if they had copies first. At three to five Egyptian pounds a tape, I could only afford one a month, and there was so much I wanted to get hold of. There were of course other Streisand studio albums and soundtracks, earlier Newton-John compilations and, a family favourite since Beirut days, Cliff Richard. (No, I was never an edgy teen.) When Newton-John's album *Totally Hot* hit the stores in Cairo in the spring of 1979, it was all that my friends and I could talk about.

The more Sadat modernized the Egyptian economy, the more Western music became readily available—and the louder the response of anti-Western, anti-government Muslim activists became. As the middle classes continued to be squeezed in favour of a merchant and entrepreneurial nouveau riche, the number of bearded men and veiled women on the streets increased. Many of them had reacted to Sadat's trip to Israel by embracing Islam. In my family it was like playing a game of hunting zombies. Whenever one of us would see an employee at a shop we frequented or a waitress at a cafe who'd "turned"—looked more identifiably Muslim—we'd report it to each other. My sisters held their ground and refused to cover up, still seeing the veil as an extreme (and déclassé) reaction. They tried as hard as they could to cling to their freedoms—and for the most part they succeeded.

Hoda worked for an ad agency that placed commercials on Egyptian television, while Ferial abandoned her master's degree when she was offered a job in a famous antique shop in a tourist resort near the pyramids. Both made decent money, but more significantly, they were independent women who followed in the footsteps of our older sister Farida, who still worked for the Liberian embassy in Cairo. I watched as they planned their work wardrobe for the whole week, occasionally arguing over a shared blouse or perfume. At the same time, Helmi was still studying law at university and rarely, if ever, made any money. Either out of spite, pride or religious piety, he'd criticize his sisters' dresses as too tight or too revealing. Their makeup made them look like whores, he'd tell them in the morning as they left for work or when they came home at the end of a long day. My sisters learned to ignore him and overcompensated by buying more clothes and makeup and staying longer at work to avoid confrontations.

But even I could sense some tension among my sisters. Because Farida got her pay in US dollars and received considerably more than Hoda or Ferial, she could afford to buy more expensive clothes. She'd spend a hundred Egyptian pounds on perfume or makeup in a single shopping trip, which was about a third of what the other two sisters made in a month. Her evening dresses for weddings and receptions were extravagant by Egyptian standards, and all my sisters could do was watch—admiringly, but with some jealousy. My mother became quite concerned at the disparity among her daughters and took it out on my father for not providing his children with more money. My father in turn became more concerned about his girls' taste for expensive fashions and accessories, which he felt would make them stand out in the more middle-class (read struggling) parts of Cairo.

At best Mohamed was overprotective, and at worst paranoid. (He was also an obsessive-compulsive who washed his hands before lunch three or four times and never left home before checking he had his wallet and whatever else he needed at least a dozen times.) Changes in Cairo fed into his paranoia. He would often talk of people following him, possibly to rob him, or would ask my mother not to let our neighbours know any details of the family's financial situation in case they broke into the apartment. Ever the sensible one, Safia would just tell him to stop obsessing ("*Batel el wiswas,*" she'd say in Arabic). She herself was equally overprotective—I was thirteen before I could go to the corner store unescorted—but, let's just say, less precious about hygiene. Anyone who shopped in Cairo's markets learned to turn a blind eye to actual conditions there. As long as she washed a piece of fruit or a vegetable once, she felt safe enough to eat it or feed it to her children.

My father's paranoia took a turn for the worse in 1978, when he bought a car and hired a driver to take us to and from school or university. He feared that cab drivers—whom we'd used for so long—would kidnap his children for ransom. He firmly believed that shifts towards radical Islam in Cairo's society had little to do with religion and everything to do with the decline in living standards. He was particularly nervous around Palestinian refugees in Cairo, whom he felt would kill one of his children for money if they could get away with it. His obsessions started to annoy my mother, who did not share them and had no frame of reference for her husband's concerns. For all we knew, Mohamed was acting crazy, but in reality events at home reflected the bigger picture in the Arab world.

Many Egyptians assumed that we, a Yemeni family, had more money than they did. As a result of this misconception we started to experience discrimination from a society that only a few years before had felt like home to us. Cab drivers charged us more if they recognized us as non-Egyptians. For my sisters, renewing work permits became an annual hassle, as the unemployment rates kept rising and the Sadat government limited the number of foreigners who could work legally in the country. The infrastructure of the country slowly crumbled, and nowhere was this more evident than in the ordeal of getting a phone line in Cairo in the late 1970s and early '80s. We lucked out in that our rented apartment came with a phone, but not many of our friends had that privilege. Well, we were lucky until the summer of 1979, when our landlord (who lived in a nearby apartment building) simply switched the phone line from our place to his. It's unfathomable to any of us now—and by that I mean my Canadian friends and my cell phone–addicted family in Yemen—to think of living for two years without a phone. But we endured just that. Public pay phones were a rarity in Cairo, so if you wanted to make a call, you had to ask in a convenience store or coffee shop whether you could use theirs in exchange for twenty or forty pence or a full Egyptian pound for long calls. Not long after he appropriated the phone line, our landlord visited my mother to let her know that the rent would be increasing by 300 percent. "Your husband works in Saudi Arabia now, so he can afford it," he told her. I can still remember my sisters pleading with him to be reasonable and to at least consider putting off any talk of an increase until Mohamed's return to Cairo. Even with my father away, none of my siblings had the authority to deal with any big financial decision. Mohamed still controlled how and where money was spent.

BY THE END OF 1979, we had further confirmation of the end of the secular era when Ayatollah Khomeini rose as Iran's spiritual leader.

I was always a sickly child. I missed weeks and weeks of school every year with one form of childhood illness or another. But that year I seemed to have caught a worse-than-usual cold, and my father was so worried about my health that he joined my mother and me on what to us was a routine visit to the doctor, a pediatrician. I was convinced that my father's reason for coming along was to find a cure for my fascination with a certain Jewish American singer.

The doctor's office was in downtown Cairo, in a historic mixed-income area known as Bab el-Louq, where its shabby art-deco buildings stand as reminders of Egypt's colonial history. The doctor himself was part of that fading Old Cairo set of rich Egyptians educated in private schools and in the United Kingdom who often lamented the socialist tendencies of post-colonial Egypt for allowing peasants (*fellaheen*) into positions of power. The medical checkup took less than ten minutes. Dr. Rashad El-Sakkar was all too familiar with my body. It was the usual: I was not eating enough vegetables and proteins. His conversation with my dad afterwards must have lasted about an hour, much to the chagrin of my mother, who wanted to go home to prepare supper.

The two old-timers got into a discussion of politics and religion. I remember the doctor being nervous about the revolutionary talk coming out of Iran. My father expressed his concern at the increasing influence of Islamic groups on municipal life in Cairo. Mosques seemed to be starting up everywhere, a backlash against the Egyptian entertainment industry for its corrupting influence, etcetera. Both men agreed that more troubles were to come. The doctor advocated the imprisonment of political Islamists, as they fostered unrest and plotted an overthrow of the state. My father, who had more experience with anti-state rebels from his Aden days, sounded a less militant tone and offered a scenario that in hindsight would be considered appeasement. "Give them 10 percent of seats in Parliament to shut them up for now," he offered.

That conversation was the first of many I'd hear my father having in the following months. Each conversation—with other doctors, neighbours, bookstore owners—confirmed that the life my siblings and I had taken for granted was coming to an end. God was suddenly in the picture. My father's fears were realized less than two years later, when members of the Muslim Brotherhood assassinated

President Sadat on October 6, 1981. As another major Arabic capital started to lose its attraction as a safe haven, my father once again began to think about relocating his family. This time, economy as well as politics had to be taken into account. As his savings were being depleted by the double blow of 1970s inflation and the early 1980s recession, and since my older siblings had all graduated from university and the younger ones would be joining them in a few years, the emphasis was on choosing a place where they could find employment. For the first time, talk of going back to Yemen became more than an idle threat. It wouldn't happen for a few more years, but it looked like the family had run out of options.

CHAPTER SIX

CAIRO

Gay

My Canadian and British friends of my age associate the 1980s high-school experience with new-wave music, shoulder pads, big hair and general flamboyance. My high school, Amoun—in Zamalek, an elite neighbourhood populated by expatriates and well-heeled Egyptians—wouldn't have registered on the cool scale, but it did not lack in local glamour. In the Zamalek enclave we could all pretend that the tide of radical Islam wasn't rising. My brothers Wahbi and Khairy were in their final years of high school when I joined them there. Amoun—named after an ancient Egyptian god—was another co-ed private school, but it seemed to attract a who's who of Cairo's acting community. I was in the same class as Sherihan—the Miley Cyrus of my generation—and, in senior years, with Salah Sarhan, now a well-known Egyptian actor whose father was one of local cinema's matinee idols from the 1950s and '60s. My friend Adham was the son of Mohamed Rushdi, a famous folksinger. I carpooled with him on the way back from school for two years. His mother would drive us home on one condition: No music by her husband in the car. "It's enough having your father at home.

Give me a break in the car," she told Adham sternly whenever he tried to play a cassette of Rushdi's music.

By sixteen, I had more or less come out as being gay—at least to myself. And if I had any lingering doubts, the movie *Xanadu* put them to rest. Music from the movie had been circulating among my group of friends for months, and when in May 1981 it opened on a Monday morning, as movies did in Egypt, I stood in a long line of kids to get a ticket at the Metro Cinema in downtown Cairo. I don't remember much about that first viewing, but the second, a mere three days later at a busy Thursday-evening show, left a lasting impression.

Most seventeen-year-old-boys watching that movie were likely turned on by the beauty of Olivia Newton-John. I, on the other hand, was deeply aroused by the long hair and short shorts of her co-star, Michael Beck, an actor whose career fizzled out faster than the musical itself. When the camera zoomed in on his face during a song called "The Fall," it all became clear to me. I still get the shivers whenever I watch that scene from that loveable, goofy musical. That's it, then, I thought: I'm a homosexual. Newton-John looked gorgeous but did nothing for me sexually. Even Gene Kelly looked sexy in that movie. A few days later I went to see it for the third time.

On my way in, I stopped at the convenience store attached to the Metro Cinema and overheard a conversation between the owner and one of his friends. The friend was asking why the theatre was so busy, to which the storeowner replied that it was an audience of fools who were headed to hell for watching *haram* (forbidden) material. He was incensed that the promotional stills next to his store featured a picture of Newton-John as a 1940s glamour girl in shorts that showed off her long bare legs. "God curse them all," he said as he handed me my change and gave me a defiant look. I knew that a movie musical wouldn't be to the taste of a devout Muslim like him, but such intolerance was frightening, and this time I couldn't enjoy the movie. What was I going to do with my life if I stayed in Egypt? How would I survive the inevitable humiliation and scandal of being gay? I couldn't be the only one who felt this way, but how could I connect with others, and if I did, how could I be sure that word wouldn't get back to my family?

There was no way I'd seek guidance from my brothers, and despite my close ties to my sisters, I couldn't confide in any of them. Just because they were more sensitive to issues of gender and discrimination didn't mean they espoused liberal views about homosexuality. Any thoughts of talking it through with my male high-school friends were laid to rest whenever we went out and they talked about nothing but women's breasts and sex with girls. I'm still not sure how I got away without being called a faggot by my friends, since I never participated in any sex-related conversations. The idea of homosexuality probably never occurred to most of them. Either that or some were protesting too much, but I didn't understand it as such at the time. I now teach seventeen- and eighteen-year-old university students, and I'm stunned at their sophisticated understanding of sexuality. I envy them. My isolation at a comparable age could have led me to a different life altogether—perhaps one of suppressing my desires and seeking refuge in strict Islam as a form of self-flagellation or cleansing.

Luckily, I had other options. My English was improving and I was able to read about homosexuality in the reference library of the British Council, where I began to make the association between being gay and the need to get out of the Middle East. But I was still a high-school student and had no means of making that happen. What I wouldn't have done to be in London or New York at the time.

((

THE ROAD TO LONDON at least got shorter by the end of 1981. My sister Faiza married for the second time and eventually settled in Liverpool, where her new husband, Hamza, a British national from Aden, ran a corner store. My mother's sister Fatima and her family had already relocated to Liverpool in the early 1970s. My dad and two of my older siblings (Helmi and Farida) had visited them in the past and brought back stories about their life in England. To my father, England had deteriorated since he'd lived there in the late 1940s; to Farida, and even for the pre-religious Helmi, it was a great place. When Hamza proposed, my father had to swallow his pride and allow his daughter to marry a shopkeeper of dubious social background. Mohamed figured it'd make his next few decisions easier with one less child to take care of.

Decisions about where to relocate—from Aden to Beirut, from Beirut to Cairo—were becoming more and more difficult as the children got older. By 1982, two more of my sisters had finished university and Helmi finally received his law degree. There was no change on the work-permit front for non-Egyptians. Mohamed's trips to Saudi Arabia were cut short as he got older and found it harder to accept condescending attitudes from local businessmen. In fact, the breaking point came in 1982, when it became clear that one of his business associates more or less expected my father to procure for him during a visit to Cairo. The businessman assumed that since our family had been living in Cairo, we'd know our way around its prostitution rings. My dad was so defeated by that point he couldn't, as the English used to say, organize a fuck in a brothel. When he politely refused and declined even to suggest where this man could go, he put some of his business contacts in jeopardy. We found out about this incident several years later, but it must have been another deciding factor for a move that would send my family down a path so different from the one we'd been on: a move back to our ancestral homeland of North Yemen and its capital, Sana'a.

In the summer of 1981, the increased rent for our Tahrir Street apartment became unmanageable for my father, who decided to find a more affordable place, even if it meant going a bit outside our usual neighbourhood. Helmi found a quiet four-bedroom apart-ment on a side street about fifteen minutes' walk from our old place. The downside was that it overlooked a busy boys' public school, so we had to cope with the noise of assemblies and the nuisance of a new generation of aggressive Egyptian kids. This was the kind of school where lower-middle-class families sent their children—a far cry from the private schools we attended. By then, and it had only been a matter of three or four years, we could see many veiled schoolteachers go in and out of the school. We could also hear some of the speeches at morning assemblies, which almost always fol-lowed a strict Islamic script about the benefit of prayers or the fool-ishness of those secular folks who were trying to undermine the rise of the Islamic voice.

Faiza's wedding, in September of the same year, served as a dis-traction from the economic stresses and political tensions. At least for her siblings. For my father, the ten-year gap between her first wedding and this one captured his deteriorating financial situation. As was the custom in Arab society, the father of the bride almost always covered the wedding costs. But Mohamed was in no position to go it alone, so he agreed with the groom to split the expenses. The groom and his family would also make all decisions about venue, food and entertainment.

The wedding turned into an explosion of bad taste, according to my still-snobbish father. My siblings and I thought it was funny, and we joked about it for months afterwards. Instead of a banquet hall in one of the major hotels in downtown Cairo—as in Faiza's first wedding—the groom booked a seedy nightclub in the dodgy entertainment area called the Pyramids Road. The area became famous for fleecing Gulf-area tourists with overpriced admission tickets and menus. The entertainment consisted of seven—count them, seven—unknown belly dancers and a couple of no-name singers. There was no shortage of food, and a huge orange-coloured wedding cake that my father wouldn't eat. In another example of the gap between my parents, my mother asked the waiters to put the leftovers in boxes to take home—to the mortification of my father, who wanted no reminder of that evening.

Looking back at this wedding in 1981, I now realize that it was the last time my parents and all of their children were under the same roof. Mohamed could no longer allow his family to live in a society that restricted his freedom and theirs to seek work and make a living. After a couple of exploratory visits to Sana'a—visits that he never enjoyed—he decided to move the family headquarters there gradually over the next year or two.

Helmi volunteered himself as a canary. He was the first to leave Cairo behind, in the fall of 1982, and start a new life in Sana'a. He had some friends to fall back on, and my uncle Hussein, my father's younger brother, had already established himself somewhat. I can't say that I was all that sad to see Helmi go. He was becoming erratic in his observance—sometimes hardline and sometimes permissive when it suited his needs. He had one set of religious rules for himself and another for his sisters. His friends had too much influence on his thinking and often made me feel self-conscious about my perceived femininity or, to put it in the proper Egyptian context, lack of manly aggression. Well before "man up" became a catchphrase in American politics, I heard its Arabic equivalent from his friends. My mother had a harder time with his departure and cried for days on end. Not only was he to go to Yemen, but he had to start his life there by fulfilling the obligatory one-year military service in President Ali Abdullah Saleh's armed forces. My sisters breathed a sigh of relief, at least temporarily, for they knew they'd follow in his footsteps soon enough.

STILL, FOR ABOUT A YEAR or so the mood in the house became relaxed and we got to enjoy the old Cairo that we loved. Two years after the assassination of Sadat, and two into Mubarak's regime, Cairo was settling into a kind of stability. Yes, incidents of terrorism took place—attacks on government buildings or Christian churches—and the streets got more dangerous late at night because of increased crime and poverty, but we felt safer than we had in Beirut and knew Cairo was a lot more modern and tolerant than Sana'a.

By the time I turned eighteen I was a high-school graduate. Unlike most of my friends and even my own siblings I had no firm plans or any real ambition to go to university. All I wanted was to get more comfortable in my skin. After floundering for a year, I applied to Ain Shams University, a left-leaning alternative institution in Cairo, to study business and economics. I didn't have the confidence to enrol in the English program after going over the first-year reading list. To me, English wasn't about literature but a gateway to life as a gay man. I even read up on the gay liberation movement in New York and San Francisco, two cities I made a pilgrimage to in 1991 just to see all the places—Christopher Street, the Castro—I'd read about as a teen in Cairo. I obtained my information about gay life in the West from second-hand weekly news and entertainment magazines like *Newsweek* and, of all titles, *People*. Once a week I went to the market in downtown Cairo, the Azbakia, where they were sold. Many American expatriates sold their old magazines, which were then lapped up by Western-media-hungry people like me. To save money I'd walk all the way there and back—an hour in each direction—and spend all I had on magazines. You got the best deals and the widest selection on Mondays, as the expatriates would clean up their apartments on Sunday and get rid of magazines they didn't want. My sisters loved looking at the ads more than the content. We couldn't believe how available and attractive everything seemed in America. We'd see ads for food and clothes and assume that was how everybody in the West must have lived. In Cairo, the idea of a supermarket was novel. A handful of them popped up in more upscale neighbour-hoods in the late 1970s and early '80s. Up to that point, all the food we consumed came from the open markets or local convenience stores that sold the staples: sugar, milk, cheese and so on. The idea of buying bread (and not buying it fresh daily) anywhere but at a bakery would have been laughable to my mother.

As we flipped through those magazines, my sisters and I wanted to sample the same types of food. We thought of the newly opened and relatively expensive McDonald's and Kentucky Fried Chicken as treats for special occasions—as did most of our circle of friends. In the hierarchy of foreign foods, however, pizza occupied the top slot. It was like nothing we ever ate, and whenever we visited friends or other families where they served it, we considered it a sign of sophistication. Most Egyptian families adapted the toppings to suit local palates, so they didn't use much pepperoni or oregano and instead opted for minced meat, hot pepper and tuna.

Raja'a and I, however, wanted to try the original pizza as we saw it in the American ads. So she and I went to a supermarket on Mousadak Street, not very far from our new family home, and searched in the frozen-food section until we found a pizza that looked most like the ones in the magazines. We first had to make sure that the pepperoni was made of beef and not ham, and when we established that, we rushed home to allow it to defrost. The instructions were in English, so I did my best to translate to Raja'a and my mother, who regarded with suspicion the idea of a frozen meal that came inside a cardboard box. To the best of our ability we followed all the instructions—including taking off the cellophane wrapping—and stuck it in the oven for forty to fifty minutes. (We didn't realize that was for cooking from frozen.) When my mother began to suspect the pizza was getting burnt, she took it out of the oven, removed the scorched crusts, cut it into slices and gathered whoever was at home to try it. She wouldn't accept it as the main meal and categorized it for now as a snack. We all took one bite and stopped. It tasted awful. I insisted that it was meant to taste that way, but my mother would have none of it. She collected all the slices, put them in a garbage bag and threw it down the chute. It was the taste of oregano that must have thrown us off. From then on, whenever we craved pizza, we had to go out or follow my mother's traditional recipe. To me it wasn't pizza; just everyday food on dough.

Aside from magazines, radio became a lifeline. I got hooked on the BBC World Service for its music programming and Voice of America, which broadcast both in English and Arabic. Immersing myself in Western culture and art made me less self-conscious about my sexuality. The connections were being made in my mind: English offered a way out; Arabic a step backward. I remember talking to myself in English as I walked home from the movies or from magazine-shopping sprees. I refused to watch Arabic movies or TV shows. As my family gathered in the living room for their daily dose of Egyptian soap operas, I retreated to the room I shared with my two brothers and listened to the radio or watched anything in English on the second TV channel. (There were only two in Egypt, and we didn't get a VCR until 1985.) I took great pride in not knowing what my mother and siblings were talking about when they discussed TV shows. And as for Arabic music, that was completely banished from my record collection. I erased all those tapes of my favourite Egyptian singer, Shadia, and used them to record American and British top-twenty hits from the radio. Thursdays were for the British singles chart countdown on the BBC; Fridays for the Billboard US one.

Three decades later, as a man in my late forties, I find it inexplicable that I turned my back on Arabic music, because I think that music is so lovely now. It comforts me and fulfils an emotional need. Maybe I'm just trying to make up for the years I rejected it. I would love to attend a concert by Shadia or Nagat El-Saghira now, both of whom retired and distanced themselves from their musical careers once they'd converted to a strict reading of Islam.

BETWEEN 1983 AND 1984, my mother, four of my sisters and my brother Khairy joined Helmi in Sana'a. It was the first time I'd lived apart from my mother, and it didn't take me long to realize that I was indeed a mama's boy. Even though she didn't speak English and was not remotely interested in my choice of music and entertainment, she never stood in the way of my enjoying them and never made a value judgement about the corrupting influence of the language or the music. Every now and then, when Khairy came home from the mosque and found me watching Western music videos on TV, he'd make a comment about how it was all an American conspiracy to get Arab youth to forget about Islam and the Palestinian cause. I just wanted to watch Wham! and, my favourite English band, Spandau Ballet.

A former English high-school teacher suggested that if I liked that culture so much, I should learn more about its history and literature, and after floundering for a couple of years, I got my act together and switched programs from business to English. I didn't necessarily think of it as a subject for a university degree but as a way to polish my English writing and as a stepping stone to finish off my education in England. Faiza was still living there and in 1984 invited me to visit.

A picture of me taken by a family friend during my first visit to London in 1984. That trip changed my life and helped me come out as a gay man.

I don't think I slept for weeks prior to my flight to Heathrow. I'd dreamed of such trip for many years. There were two small obstacles to overcome, however: getting a UK visa and my father's approval (and some money). My first application for an entry visa was turned down because I hadn't bought a return ticket. I was crushed, but once I re-submitted the application with the ticket (which my brother-in-law paid for in Liverpool), I was given a single-entry visa. Getting Mohamed's approval and financial support was far more complicated. He'd made it clear that he worried about my losing my way completely if I was exposed to more Western culture. He thought I'd be brainwashed and find life back in Cairo or Yemen too restrictive. He relented only after Faiza promised she'd look after me and not let me out alone.

Finally, I thought, I was getting to go to London, not realizing that Liverpool was three hours away by train—and, more disappointingly, not knowing that Faiza and my aunt lived only in England by name. When I arrived in Liverpool, I discovered they still listened to Arabic music, watched Arabic films, cooked Arabic food and socialized only with other Arabs. Visiting my aunt's house in the multi-ethnic neighbourhood of Granby felt like I had never left the Middle East—except the streets were full of Asian and black people as well, all of whom kept to themselves. Even with part of my family living in England, I had to get away from them. I wanted to see the real England, so I hit record and book stores for hours during the day and was glued to the TV at night. I bought (and hid) my first copy of a gay magazine and daydreamed about a point in my life where I didn't have to read it secretly late at night. But it would be four years, and another summer visit to England, before that would happen.

When I returned to Cairo after that first visit, and as he'd predicted, my father and I started to argue much more. I'd tasted freedom and wanted more of it. As he travelled back and forth between Sana'a and Cairo to check in on us, he got stricter and stricter. He disapproved of me going out with friends late at night and always questioned their background. If you grew up in the Middle East, you got used to controlling parents, but Mohamed's interference suggested one of two things: his fear that I'd be experimenting sexually in the age of AIDS or, in a more Freudian twist, resentment towards me for becoming a better speaker and writer of English, a language in which he was as good as a native speaker. With my mother and most of my sisters in Yemen now, there was no buffer between the two of us.

He was right about the sexual experimentation. The visit to England gave me a confidence boost and I found the courage to call the Liverpool gay helpline and ask for information on finding other gay men in Cairo. Much to my surprise, the helpful operator said that the international gay guide *Spartacus* listed some bars in downtown Cairo as meeting places. "Are you sure?" I asked in disbelief. It was hard for me to imagine the possibility of meeting other people publically who felt the same way that I did, given how isolated my early years as a gay teen had been. "Well, the Tavern at the Cairo Nile Hilton comes up in various guides," he replied. I knew the hotel but had no idea where that tavern was, or what to do when I got there.

Though I was already twenty, I was very naive and inexperienced. But even in the Cairo of 1984 the possibility of meeting gay men, particularly Westerners, was too big an attraction for me to miss. I remember going to a fancy hair salon in Cairo and asking the stylist to straighten my long hair with a flat iron. I wore my best wool sweater and cotton pants—I was anything but fashionable—and walked to the Nile Hilton in Tahrir Square, a landmark in Cairo since 1959. Once I identified the Tavern pub, I circled its doors a few times before I walked in. When I did, I had no idea what to expect. There was an Australian lounge singer doing a version of "Don't Cry Out Loud," a few leather seats, a big screen that divided the place into two and a rectangular bar with a terrifyingly stern-looking Egyptian barman. I had never until then consumed any alcohol, and when I found a seat at the bar, I couldn't think of anything to order except a gin and tonic because I'd heard of it in

American movies. I had no idea what it would taste like. I began sipping it—it didn't taste so bad—and looking around. To my horror I immediately spotted a family friend, who either didn't recognize me or chose to ignore me. I began to connect the dots. So, lots of men on their own or talking to other men. Very few women, Egyptian or Western. The men were all trying to catch each other's eye. Older white men. Younger Egyptians. Lots of furtive glances and nervous laughter. The lounge singer started humming "Sometimes When We Touch," which I had never heard before but immediately thought the most romantic song ever.

Then it happened. A Swiss businessman said hello and raised his glass. I thought he'd probably mixed me up with the waiter and was just ordering another drink. I don't remember how we got talking, but it would be the very first time I ever chatted in person to another human being who identified himself as gay. It would be the start of many Thursday-night encounters at the Nile Hilton Tavern. I loved nothing more than being chatted up and seduced by older Western or Egyptian men. It became a sport, and I'd always felt I'd lost the game if I wasn't invited back to a hotel room or at least got a ride home and a fondle in the car with one of the Egyptian businessmen, who were almost always married and couldn't take me home anyway. Not that it was always that easy. I had nightmares about being caught or contracting HIV, which was just beginning to be the great epidemic that would define sexuality in the 1980s. But the pleasures outweighed the restlessness and fears—including the very real threat of being arrested and charged with sodomy. Building a network of Egyptian and expatriate gays changed my life. I wasn't alone, and even if I still lived a secretive life, I had some older men to guide me through it.

Ahmad, a tailor, and his boyfriend, Bill, an American high-school teacher, took me under their wing. Both were in their late thirties and communicated largely in broken English and Arabic. Ahmad came from a poor working-class background and his English was largely picked up from previous sexual encounters with other Americans and Brits. Occasionally, I'd act as a translator between the two. I couldn't have been happier. They introduced me to Cairo's authentic gay scene—as opposed to the one based on meeting foreigners in hotels—which centred around a seedy part of the city known as Haret Abu Ali. Of the many chapters in my life, this one seems the most surreal to me now. It was like discovering that a lost city we'd only heard of in fables existed all along and was just a cab ride away. Belly dancers who'd seen better days had ended up there performing in cabarets for a clientele of wisecracking tough Egyptians and groups of gay men. Westerners would come as guests of the Egyptian gay men for the novelty factor, but you had to understand Egyptian Arabic to make the most of the comedy acts or the music. Even though I hated that kind of music, I quickly appreciated its camp value and its meaning as part of the Egyptian gay experience. I'd always loved belly dancing anyway and the religious crackdown in Egypt meant that there were fewer and fewer dancers. For a brief moment, I was living in a Cairo that recalled the golden days of the 1950s and early '60s that I saw on TV.

Of course it wouldn't last.

IN 1986 MOHAMED INSISTED on relocating the remaining members of his family to Sana'a. Keeping two households had become too big a financial burden for him. I didn't need to visit Sana'a to know I wouldn't be happy there—not after I'd finally settled into Cairo's underground gay scene. I saw what living there was doing to my sisters when they visited the family home in Cairo on their summer vacations. For one thing, they complained about life in Sana'a all the time. After the relative freedom they grew up in, they were having to adjust to a society where women had to cover their heads and wear an abaya—a black, loose-fitting coat to hide the contours of the body. For the first time, they experienced full-blown misogyny and discrimination, both as women and as Aden-born Yemeni citizens. Sana'a of the 1980s was a very closed society and rarely welcomed strangers. To the average Sana'a male, women from Aden who were educated in places like Beirut and Cairo were loose by definition. I don't think that attitude has shifted much in the past thirty years, despite all the uprisings and anti-government protests.

On a political level, President Saleh ran the country like a private club and a police state. My sister Ferial was under security investigation for many months and denied an identity card—the most essential document a Yemeni citizen needs—because she was more outspoken and independent than my other sisters. The rest experienced various but milder forms of intimidation and harassment before they could work legally.

The combination of living in Yemen, an extremely conservative society, and being under my father's and brother's thumbs, both of whom were equally rigid by now, meant that my sisters had to internalize the dominant culture's attitude towards women. "What's the use?" Hoda would tell me when I suggested she should relax a little now that she was visiting Cairo, "I'm going back to prison in a few weeks." It was both a physical and psychological prison. When we went out for lunch or dinner in Cairo, I noticed that my sisters left it up to me to do all the ordering and talking with waiters. Just a few years before, I'd left those decisions to them. They surrendered their voices to the nearest male relative, which on those occasions meant me. When we went shopping, they'd gravitate towards the most conservative clothes and avoid items that could give the wrong signals—high heels, bright colours—even if they covered whatever they wore with the abaya. How different were these shopping trips from the times we looked for bikinis for the summer season together.

As a man, I knew I'd probably fare better than my sisters in Yemen's male-dominated society. It's a privilege to be a man there, period. But not a gay man. Leaving Cairo now would be one thing; leaving it for Sana'a another.

I didn't have a choice. I'd failed to secure any scholarship to complete my studies abroad, and all the flirting and sleeping around hadn't landed me a partner who might whisk me off to somewhere in the West. I had flings and silly crushes but no relationships.

After fifteen years it was time to say goodbye to Cairo. My mother flew back from Yemen to help with selling the furniture and to pack years and years of clothes and collectables. When she and my sisters had departed for Yemen a few years earlier, they had left most of their belongings in Cairo. Perhaps they were secretly hoping they'd return after a year or two of Sana'a. Maybe if they left some clothes in Cairo, Yemen wouldn't seem so permanent.

Wahbi and I were responsible for arranging the furniture sale and using the proceeds to buy our plane tickets. Neither of us was any good at that sort of transaction and the shrewd second-hand furniture dealers saw through us. One after another they made lowball offers—everything for three or four hundred Egyptian pounds—hardly enough to pay for one ticket, let alone two. It was a handy reminder of the gap between us as Yemeni expatriates and Egyptians and, to my brother, another reason why we should leave. We saw ourselves as part of Cairo society, and they saw us as rich Arabs to whom a few hundred pounds would make no difference.

Back then, you didn't just call a second-hand store and ask them to come and have a look; you actually had to go there and bring the owner or an employee home. When I was asked to bring back a furniture seller from the working-class neighbourhood of Imbaba, I took a taxi there and expected a ride back in the shop owner's truck. I did get a ride back. On a donkey cart. I had seen them on the streets of Cairo before and in movies but never expected to ride in one. I don't know if I ever told any of my friends in Cairo about that experience. To me now, it's just another quirky Cairo story. At the time, I was mortified. When we eventually made it to our street, the salesman, as expected, made an even lower offer than the rest.

That's when my mother stepped in. Safia may have been illiterate, but she knew how to bargain, having shopped in Cairo's food markets for years. When the salesman was about to stage the first of his many walkouts to force us into accepting his offer, Safia made him a counter-offer. I can't remember the exact figure, but it was above what we told her two airline tickets to Sana'a would cost. She asked him to accept it now and she'd throw in some clothes— including some of her fur coats, which she hadn't worn since the early 1970s—or he could leave right away and not come back. A minute or two later we had a deal. Cash in hand. For about a week or so, we had no furniture except the beds, which the seller returned to pick up on the day we left for Sana'a.

I've taken many plane rides before and since and have moved from continent to continent in the last two decades, but nothing came close to how frightened I felt holding that one-way ticket from Cairo to Sana'a. What would I do in Yemen, and what would Yemen, a country that punished homosexuality with public hanging or lashings, do to a twenty-two-year-old gay man like me?

CHAPTER SEVEN

SANA'A

Ancestral

It couldn't have begun on a worse note. At the Customs counter of Sana'a International Airport in the fall of 1986, a severe-looking officer with a military overcoat on top of traditional Yemeni clothing insisted on examining a box marked in Cairo as "Heavy." It contained two years' worth of the British pop music magazine *Record Mirror,* which my sister had been sending to me from Liverpool. They were my window into British and American pop music, especially as each issue carried the UK and US album and singles charts. Back in Cairo, my friends would take turns reading old issues and making note of upcoming album releases. The magazine always featured flamboyant indie acts on the cover, men with makeup or women dressed in skimpy clothing: the Cure, Lloyd Cole and the Commotions, Madonna.

"This goes against our traditions as a Muslim country," the Customs officer said, and told me he'd confiscate all copies. "Shame on you for bringing this to our land," he added as he flipped through them, himself transfixed. Wahbi insisted that they were for private use, but the officer countered that it made no difference. A few

supplicating "*ma'lesh*," never minds, and "*yallahs*," come ons, later
and I made it out with my magazines. It never even occurred to me
that a general-interest music magazine would be considered por-
nographic in Yemen, but the experience coloured my perception
of our so-called ancestral homeland before I even left the airport.
"You'll get used to it," my mother told me later the same day. It
wasn't long before I discovered that the full sentence should have
gone something like, You'll get used to it, but you'll not necessarily
like it.

Culture shocks are meant to happen when you take an indi-
vidual from his native environment and drop him onto completely
unfamiliar ground. By all rights, Yemen shouldn't have been so
culturally alien. Unlike Aden, however, which was a port city and
colonial melting pot, Sana'a had isolated itself from the world for
much of the twentieth century. It was literally a gated community,
with the historic Bab al Yemen, the Gate of Yemen, closing off the
city at night to visitors in the old days. Nearly twenty-five years since
the troops of Gamal Abdel Nasser helped local republicans liber-
ate the country from the pseudo-monarchist rule of the Sayyids,
or the Masters, the city, like the country as a whole, was divided
along the lines of those who wanted to modernize it in the style of
the Gulf states and those who fought to keep it in a time capsule—
somewhere between the late Victorian and early modern eras. Judging from the increasing number of businesses, cars and electronics
stores, the modernizing faction was winning. Just about.

Getting used to Yemen while resenting it captured the mood at
our reunited family home. It had been just three to four years since
my older siblings left Cairo, but within days of arriving in Sana'a I
noticed a disturbing family dynamic. Our new residence was two
separate apartments in a detached house in the then-quiet Hasaba
district, a short bus ride away from Sana'a's own Tahrir Square and

the historic Old City. (The Hasaba is the nerve centre of the student protests that escalated into a civil war in 2011.) Helmi had got married the year before and lived with his wife and, shortly after my arrival, his first child in the family home. My sister Ferial worked in the USAID as an education officer, while Raja'a landed a job as a librarian in Sana'a University. Hoda had changed jobs as an executive assistant a number of times but was settling in at the main local administrative offices and factory of 7UP. Hanna had started a new job as a social worker in a government-run school and was married to a man who mainly showed up for work to collect his paycheque, which, in Yemen, literally meant taking your salary in cash at the counter. I always saw it as a sign of how strange and yet incredibly safe Sana'a was that on payday men and women would carry around plastic bags containing wads of cash. No one feared being mugged.

I can't say my sisters weren't independent financially. The country was generous to them in that respect. This was Yemen before the inflation of the 1990s and the economic decline of the last two decades of President Saleh's rule. The US dollar was worth about five Yemeni riyals, so the purchasing power of the professional class—which, legitimately, became our status in the world now—was high. (At the time of my writing this book, the US dollar stands at 250 riyals, which explains why the country is routinely described as one of the poorest in the Arab world.) But while they gained financially, my sisters lost some serious ground in terms of social and intellectual independence. Whether they liked it or not, they had to wear headscarves and abayas and learn not to engage in arguments in public spaces with, say, shopkeepers or taxi drivers. Women didn't speak much in Yemen, as their voices might be too tempting for men, and limited their socializing to home gatherings with other women. My sisters, for example, couldn't just sit in a restaurant and eat a meal together without a male companion. Yemenis considered it both dangerous and suspicious for women to walk alone at night. Even if my sisters had to walk just a few blocks home after a house party, they'd take a cab or call me or my brother to accompany them. In effect, my main role for the first few months was to chaperone them. The culture in general smacked of centuries-old hypocrisies and a fear of women. Even the few liberal men we knew, people who had once lived in Cairo or Beirut, or had got their education in the UK or the US, would say in public all the right things about women's equality and freedom but act like prison guards to their own wives and sisters. I remember, a day or two after arriving in Sana'a, opening my arms to my cousin Yousra, who was my favourite as a child and like a sister to me, only to be rebuffed with a handshake—a warm handshake, but a sign that I could no longer hug my own cousin in this society.

Another new reality. As sad as I was to see my beloved sisters relegated to far-from-equal status, I had my own struggles to deal with. Where was I? Who were these people who ate green leaves called khat, storing it in their mouths before spitting it all out in a bowl? The khat-chewing sessions in the afternoons, especially on Thursdays, emerged as the major social activity of men and women in Sana'a. If you wanted to get ahead and network, you had to spend hundreds of riyals every week buying and sharing the stuff. I took an instant aversion to it, which, my brother Khairy always reminded me, was my biggest mistake and the main reason I didn't feel at home in Yemen. Given that it's a mild form of narcotic, I see both the point and the irony of his comment. You needed to be on a high to come to terms with the country's many lows. Not even the homoeroticism of an all-male gathering could tempt me.

For the first few days Wahbi and I walked around like two tourists on an exotic vacation. My father encouraged us to familiarize ourselves with our ancestral land. "This is where you'll make a career without having to beg for a work permit from the Egyptians," Mohamed would tell us. I still felt out of place and longed to return to Cairo, at least to my new gay life. Not all the differences were emotional, though. I genuinely had trouble deciphering the dialect of people from Sana'a, and almost always felt like bringing one of my cousins or siblings who had been there for a while as an interpreter. Even when I walked alone and caught another man's eyes, I'd look away in fear.

I figured there'd be no Nile Hilton Tavern there, and even if there was one, I wouldn't dare go inside. I'd only been sexually active for two years, and now I had to be celibate again. It didn't help that my cousins and even my own siblings made my difficulty at adjusting a running gag during social gatherings. At a traditional Yemeni restaurant, I asked to see a menu, which had my cousin Taha in tears laughing. There was no menu. The waiter just told you what the kitchen could do today and you ordered one of the items he mentioned. Suddenly, I was the odd one out even within the family. I was spoiled, I was told. Toughen up, Helmi advised, or I'd find it impossible to make my way in Sana'a. But I wanted to make my way out of this society, not into it. Adapting was my only choice, however, and despite the profound sadness of those early days, some bright spots followed.

Part of me enjoyed the quaintness of Sana'a. Whole districts felt like a movie set for a period piece, circa the seventeenth century, perhaps one of those racist Hollywood movies from the 1940s, *Road to Morocco,* or something with "Ali Baba" in the title. The feeling of being a tourist in my own land offered temporary relief from the pain of losing Cairo. At night, Sana'a became quiet and strangely serene. The din of buses, speeding cars and carousing youth that defined nightlife in Cairo was replaced by silence. You would see very little traffic after 9 p.m., apart from the usual central security

Jeeps with armed soldiers roaming the streets. I wasn't sure what they were trying to detect or deter. Random violence and break-ins were unheard of. As locals explained to us, the patrols were just the president's way of imprinting his security apparatus on the brains of the citizens—just in case they got any ideas. By that point President Saleh had been in power for nearly eight years, the latest Yemeni president after assassinations had finished off his two predecessors. Political violence was to be expected in a country that was largely tribal (as Yemen is to this day). That explained the extra measures of security in an otherwise peaceful country.

Despite my father's promises and my brother's assurances, as Yemenis from Aden we were treated as second-class citizens. To get the coveted Yemeni identity card we had to go through a long and humiliating application process. Because Wahbi and I were the last in the family to seek work in Sana'a, we went through this Orwellian experience together. In an old building that was cut off from the street by a large metal gate, through which one applicant at a time was let in, we filled in one form after another. The questions ranged from the basic data—birthdate, education, passport number—to what could only be described as the stuff of dystopian fiction. What, if any, political or social organizations had we joined in the last ten years? Who had we mixed with socially in the last few years? (This was a question I had no intention of answering truthfully. "Lots of gay Egyptians and Westerners" was not the sort of response you wrote.) Almost each application included a request for a brief synopsis of about ten or fifteen lines of our lives so far. It was humiliating. "We all had to go through it," Helmi would tell me, as if that made it more comforting. It was just as well I had such low expectations going into that country.

When I finally had an "interview" with a security agent, I was horrified by how much he knew about my brothers and sisters. He

had a family file where he had collected our "bios" and proceeded
to quiz me as if to see if I or any of my siblings had lied to him.
These interviews always took place in offices that were brightly lit
or had big windows. The contrast between the bright setting and the
dark nature of the interview was deliberate, I think. It signalled that
everything was being conducted in the open. There were no secrets,
and you couldn't complain to anyone, even if you wanted. This was
Yemeni government business. Like it or leave it.

WITHIN WEEKS I FOUND MYSELF involved in that world of internal security in a more direct way. As a Yemeni I had to spend one
year in a government agency as part of my military service. After a
few days of mock training and bribing my way out of spending the
night in a dormitory, and given that I spoke good English, I was
assigned the role of translator and interpreter for the main com-
manders in the central security unit. I wasn't quite sure why they
needed a translator there, but I figured it'd be a better way of performing my service than patrolling the streets or guarding foreign
embassies, something that Helmi and Khairy had to do. I look with
amazement at a picture of me in green military uniform that Khairy
took during my first week of service. Somehow, I think, the family
wanted visual proof of my masculinity and place in Yemeni society
as a man. I thought of it more or less as male drag in the style of the
Village People or Frankie Goes to Hollywood.

"Time will pass so quickly," my mother would tell me. And
before I knew it, I fell into a routine. I got up at five thirty in the
morning, reported for duty by seven and returned home at two
in the afternoon in time for lunch. As soon as I could, I took off
the uniform and started listening to Streisand and watching old
videos of 1980s pop that I'd taped off Egyptian TV. Like my own

father, who'd mastered the art of denial over many years after we were kicked out of Aden, I thought it wouldn't be long before I went back to Cairo—or at the very least got out of Yemen. Even as Cairo was becoming more conservative and the influence of the Muslim Brotherhood threatened its secular society, it still worked as largely a liberal society. I had female friends there with whom I socialized, and of course a network of gay friends—two avenues of connection that were impossible for me in Sana'a.

My brother Khairy took this picture of me wearing my military uniform in 1988 with his new Polaroid camera. To me, the uniform was drag; to him, a symbol of masculinity.

I found it extremely difficult to make friends in Sana'a, so I spent more time with my sisters at home and experienced the country through their eyes as much as mine. On days when the chief commanding officer I reported to was out of the country, I skipped work and instead accompanied either Hoda or Ferial to work. Hoda worked in a very Yemeni office environment, while Ferial's job was predominantly with Americans in the USAID office. I'd help Hoda with translation or paperwork, and in the offices of USAID I mainly read American magazines and *USA Today*. The difference in how the two women were treated opened my eyes to the discrimination in that society. Hoda was talked down to by her male co-workers, who often told her how to do her job, while Ferial was given a great deal of freedom and relied on as a local woman who knew Yemeni society. Hoda took the discrimination in stride and made the most of the job. She couldn't afford not to work.

FIVE YEARS INTO HIS NEW LIFE in Yemen, my father had yet to make any major business deals or bring in an income. As was his habit in Cairo, he spent hours every day typing up letters and making calls that usually led to nothing. I was struck by his lack of compassion for his own daughters. When we lived in Beirut and Cairo, Mohamed championed his beautiful daughters and took pride in their education and freedom. He often reminded us of the freedoms he gave his daughters and expected them to respect his trust. In Yemen, he turned a blind eye to their experiences as second-class citizens. Every now and then he'd admit that this was a backward society, but that admission almost always came with resigned acceptance of it as a fact.

What made Yemen even harder as a new home was the strict adherence to Islam across the different classes and communities. It became impossible not to organize the day according to the five calls to prayer—at dawn, noon, afternoon, sunset and night—since everybody else worked around them. And it wasn't just any kind of Islam but a strict Zaidi version that applied sharia law. (As late as 1987, public hanging or flogging in a designated area of the city centre passed for entertainment for some watchers.) When word got out that two men who were found "sodomizing" were scheduled to be flogged after Friday prayers, I felt physically ill. The feeling only intensified when I heard Helmi's reaction. They deserved it, he said nonchalantly. Yemen hardened the attitudes of an already observant brother and worked hard on wearing down my sisters' defences. By then, we had a strict rule in the house: No man, not even a male cousin or other close relative, could come into the living room unless my sisters were all covered up or at least wearing long-sleeved dresses. The gender apartheid operated outside and inside with equal rigour. The architecture of Yemeni homes accommodated this separation. Almost all residences had two entry doors: one that led to the family living room and another directly to the *diwan,* or salon, which stayed mostly empty and in which men were invited to sit until the coast was clear, so to speak. Repairmen or labourers had to wait outside, and if they needed to go through the living quarters, they had to avoid any eye contact with the women.

Only ten years before, the same women were splashing in their bikinis in Alexandria.

I internalized all of these customs rather quickly, but never felt at home with them. I acted my way through life as if I were a different person. Or as if I were two people: one who would show up for work and deal with gruff military men whose strong Sana'ani dialect I still had difficulty understanding; the other who would spend the evening writing to his Cairo and international friends—my school friend Nancy had moved to Chicago a year before to join her sister, and a buddy from the Nile Hilton Tavern had moved back to Bournemouth, England—and dreaming of a getaway.

EVEN IF I COULD LEAVE Yemen, it wouldn't be for a few more months, as there was no cutting short my military service. It wasn't long before I understood the central security unit's need for an in-house translator. Most of my work was to translate business letters and proposals as well as catalogues from international arms manufacturers and dealers. The office's main resource was an English-Arabic technical dictionary, which I consulted regularly, since not all my language training could have prepared me for translating the specifications for grenades or "city-friendly" military tanks (tanks that could be rolled out on streets without leaving fractures or craters in the asphalt). While I reported directly to a captain, most meetings were run by the head of the security apparatus, Mohammed Abdullah Saleh, the president's older brother. Some of what I and another colleague had to translate were personal medical reports, and when needed I'd act as English teacher to any of Mohammed Saleh's extended family. As long as I said yes and never argued, I was fine. Although there were incidents where I left early without permission or made translation errors and was punished the next morning by being forced to do push-ups in the courtyard to the captain's taunts.

Political and personal survival was all I could think of. With my military service out of the way, I'd be able to do whatever I wanted. And what I wanted was to get out of that country as fast as humanly possible. I knew that would mean leaving my family behind, including my mother and sisters, with whom I was closer now that I shared their sense of entrapment. Safia was in her mid-fifties by then, and four years in Yemen had taken a toll on her health and looks. Her rheumatism got more severe and developed into arthritis. She found it hard to stand up for long or take steps up or down in the family home. In effect, at just fifty-six, she was housebound. There were not that many places anyway for her to visit; my sisters did the grocery shopping, and since women had few public spaces to mingle, if Safia went out at all she just visited other relatives or family friends—from one living room to another. Even Victorian women got to go to balls, I thought. Her life, like that of her daughters, had changed dramatically. The Safia who'd walked up and down Cairo's markets, bargaining down fruit and vegetable sellers and chatting with clerks in the haberdashery shop, was gone. To me it was like watching the life drain out of one woman after another in the family.

In 1988, I was invited to a social gathering with a group of men from Sana'a who were, like me, fulfilling their military service. I have no recollection of their names. As I look at the picture, I barely recognize myself—I'm sitting down, far left—let alone the others.

As a man, I knew at least that I had the gender advantage in Sana'a. I could go out wherever I wished, and if I chose to travel, I didn't need a male companion's approval. When my sisters would visit us in Cairo, my brother accompanied them to the Sana'a airport to sign off on documents to indicate his approval of their travel plans.

"You're lucky to be a man," my sister Raja'a—who, like me, loved American movies and grew up adoring Tom Jones—would tell me. She was married for one year to a Yemeni man who lived in Jeddah, Saudi Arabia, and had a daughter in 1987 before her husband more or less abandoned her and married another woman. Her life was effectively ruined—a single, divorced mother at twenty-eight had few prospects in Sana'a's ultraconservative society. It took her almost three years to get a divorce in absentia. She never saw her husband again.

My sister Hanna was also unhappy with her domestic situation, having been forced into marriage with a man she didn't know well. Both sisters grew up watching romantic Egyptian and Hollywood movies and felt betrayed by what the move to Yemen had done to their dreams of independent and free lives. Watching those same movies or listening to the same music in their company at times became unbearable as they quietly wept, doing their best to hide their tears.

Slowly, both sisters started to turn to religion as a way of licking their wounds. They insisted that they found praying or reading the Quran to be comforting, that it didn't mean they were becoming hardline or intolerant like many other people around them. It seemed to be a coping mechanism. Naturally, Helmi was supportive of their discovery of Islam and praised them for following their rightful path in life. Any attempt on my part to get them to return to our secular roots would have been seen as interference. My two other sisters, Hoda and Ferial, were unmarried and seemed to have resisted the tide of sudden religiosity for now. They talked of trying and failing to get out of Yemen. Hoda was engaged briefly to an Egyptian and was secretly hoping he'd relocate to Cairo so she could follow him. Ferial would go on any business trip or to any conference the USAID would send her. But despite all these escape attempts, they eventually accepted Sana'a as their home. "We'll be buried here," Hoda would say, part in jest, part in desperation.

I was determined not to fall into the same trap. I felt guilty for turning my back on them and plotting my exit strategy without them. But it was easier that way. My fate couldn't be the same as theirs. My father sensed what was happening and tried to dissuade me from any plans to immigrate or study abroad. It'll break your mother's heart, he cautioned. I knew that, but it was either her heart or mine. I didn't have the luxury of saving both.

But just as things were getting serious, along came some moments of comic relief. Because the number of women outnumbered men in Yemeni society, it wasn't that uncommon for match-makers to visit family homes with details of brides who might make suitable matches for the men in well-to-do households—sometimes even married males, as Muslim men have the right to marry up to four, although that remains a rare arrangement. Word must have got out that Wahbi and I were single and in our twenties, even though he was still in university and I had no job. I'd get a kick out of hearing out various descriptions of women—they were always beautiful and dutiful—who might one day make me a happy and contented man. Now that I've lived in the West for nearly a quarter of a century, I look back at that phase of life as if I'm watching a Bollywood movie in my head where my family and I played the leads.

Traditionally, the matchmakers visited on Friday evening, which clashed with my favourite radio show on Voice of America, featuring the countdown of the *Billboard* Top 20 singles chart. I realize it must sound strange to be listening to which song climbed to Number 1 in the United States with one ear and marriage plans involving complete strangers with the other. But I was used to living a double life by then. My brother and I sat through the descriptions of the women just to please the matchmakers. Even my sisters and my mother—bless them—didn't approve of being married that way and merely humoured the matchmakers.

I often wondered if any of my sisters had by then guessed that I wasn't interested in women at all. Perhaps they were just trying to protect me or play the game by going through the motions with the matchmakers. It would throw my brother and father off my gay scent for a little while at least.

EVEN THOUGH FERIAL worked in the USAID, I didn't stand a chance of continuing my studies in the United States. Most of the scholarships offered by the US government were in effect bribes for the children of rich and powerful business people and the ruling class in exchange for favourable contracts for American businesses or for gaining political ground in the region. Besides, most of the scholarships focused on science and technology, making my proposed English major an even longer shot. Britain, therefore, seemed a more manageable destination. The local British Council offered a range of scholarships that had no specific area of study attached to them. But those, too, were competitive and usually came with a long waiting list. I needed to find a shortcut. If I waited too long in Yemen, perhaps I'd follow in my siblings' defeatist footsteps.

Luckily, a teaching-assistant position in an English language program at Sana'a University opened up. I knew at the interview that I'd got the job since the interview committee, made up of English and American professors, commented on my English proficiency. Step one accomplished. I could network with the British and American staff and seek advice or, more importantly, reference letters. I didn't have much to do during the day, as most classes were in the evening, so I started to make a list of all the great works of English literature that I hadn't read and went through them one by one at the British Council library. It all sounds very colonial, even to my ears now: reading Jane Austen or Charles Dickens in Yemen during the monsoon season, in the library of the British Council. This took place at a time before terrorism and attacks on Western targets were to define Yemen in the eyes of the world. The British Council was in an old house on a side street in Sana'a's downtown. The only security was an old befuddled Yemeni guard whom I got to know well that year. All you needed was to show your membership card. He often left his post to attend prayers, so you could walk in without a card if you timed your visit right. His son, then about nine or ten, filled in for him when he got sick.

It was, in retrospect, a charmed life. The only reminders that I was in Yemen while inside the British Council were the calls to prayers. The Council also gave away old copies of the *Times* and *Daily Telegraph*, my introduction to serious journalism in English and my window into social, especially gay, life in the UK. I read whatever I could lay my hands on: magazines, newspapers, books. As long as it was written in English, I'd read it. English was, and would continue to be, my escape route from Yemen, my path to an openly gay life. I was certain of it. After all, English had already served me well in that regard in Egypt.

I called that one right. It wasn't long before I impressed the head of the school, an older English gentleman who'd taught in several Third World countries. He told me about a private scholarship that the Council offered a Yemeni applicant who was deemed worthy of support and a chance at a British education. He'd talk to the right people about it and get back to me. In a way, I thought it was too good to be true, too easy to happen that quickly. A few weeks later, I had a firm offer of financial support if I landed a place at a British institution where I could quickly get a B.A. equivalency and study for a master's in English. It was at most a two-year grant, after which I had to return to Sana'a. Since I had no other offers and stood no realistic chance of getting anything near as generous, I accepted, without telling anyone in my family. Two years in Britain would give me enough time to plan ahead. From there I could go to the States. Imagine: living in New York. One thing I had no intention of doing was going back to Yemen. After applying to several universities, I accepted the first offer I got, from Keele University in Staffordshire, not even knowing where it was on the map. Without a place, I had no scholarship, or I'd have to wait another full year. I had been in Yemen for about sixteen months and I just couldn't stand being there (and being celibate) for another year.

Now came the hard part. Telling my mother that I'd be away for at least two years. I knew how upset she'd be. She'd already hinted that the only thing that kept her going in Sana'a was having her children close by. Her husband provided no comfort. Two decades of trying and failing to restart his business had turned Mohamed into a bitter and argumentative man. In the past he could claim that Lebanese and Egyptian business ethics didn't suit his. Now, in his home country, what was his excuse? I don't think Mohamed or Safia had said a word to each other in over a year. After more than forty years of marriage, it was as if they had separated. They'd survived his womanizing, her inability to give him a son until the fifth pregnancy, expulsion from Aden and exodus from Beirut and Cairo, but not Sana'a. Mohamed had his own quarters in the house, and we rarely saw him, anyway. To leave my mother now, when she probably needed me the most, would be extremely selfish. I tested out the idea by telling her that I might be going for some training in the UK for a few weeks. She seemed pleased for me and added that I could visit Faiza and my aunt in Liverpool. Then I dropped the bomb. "Well, I may also go for a full year or two." To my surprise, she didn't seem to mind. She knew how unhappy I was in Sana'a. She said one word that captured it all: *ihrab*, escape. I was stunned. I expected tears and strong opposition. I expected her to beg me to forget about the scholarship and stay close to the family. But after a short silence she repeated that word: escape.

Run for your life, she might have added. Later she told me that the news devastated her, but she'd learned to give priority to her children's happiness. As I needed a bit more cash to get me through the transition, she sold her favourite gold bracelet, a family heirloom, to help me buy some sterling in the old market in Sana'a. We had to keep it a secret, as even my sisters would have thought it a major sacrifice and talked her out of it. I never got around to buying her a replacement bracelet. I still regret it.

Leaving my sisters was more difficult. Plotting my escape had been easy; it had all seemed so remote and far-fetched. It was real now. As a moderate male voice in the family, I knew that my sisters would lose an important ally. Yemen was the end of the line for them. I tried to rationalize it. Well, if they, too, studied hard they might have received scholarships and left the country. Or if they married rich, they could travel out of Yemen more often. It didn't matter much in the end. I managed to break away because I wanted it so badly and because I was a man. While they were all happy for me, they knew that baby brother Kamal would be leaving the nest for good, abandoning them to look after two parents who lived in a state of indifference to each other.

My sisters' capacity for sacrifice was (and still is) something I accepted as fact but could never understand. I don't do sacrifice, unless it's a temporary measure to achieve a higher goal down the road. Certainly, part of their ability to suffer and sacrifice came from gender expectations in that society, but I think a bigger part simply had to do with life in Yemen. In a world that cut choices short for women, sacrifice gave you something to do—it was an achievement of a sort, a choice, so to speak.

I spent my last few weeks in Sana'a both counting the days and wishing time would go slowly. I couldn't wait to get out, but wanted to stay longer with my mother and sisters. I knew I had no intention of ever going back. Somehow I was less attached to my brothers and father. Being gay made me side with the women in the family and stop acting like a man around the house. That said, there was little evidence of machismo around the family home on my last night in Sana'a. Tears, hugs, advice. Helmi gave me a copy of the Quran to keep with me at all times for protection. I left it at home. My father repeated one of his stories from his time in London after the Second World War. My mother sobbed quietly in the kitchen as my sisters took turns calming her down.

I had to be strong. Sentimentality would hold me back. I was finally going to be doing what I'd dreamed of for years: living in England and possibly openly as a gay man.

CHAPTER EIGHT

ENGLAND

Escape

I kept looking at the UK visa stamped on my passport. My letter from the British Council was tucked into the inside pocket of the oversized black jacket I'd bought from a street vendor in Sana'a a few days earlier. I wanted to make sure that neither my passport nor that letter could slip out, so I looked for a jacket with a button on the inside pocket until I found one. It didn't matter that it was two sizes too big for what was then my very thin body. I couldn't risk losing the documents and delaying my journey to England or being prevented from entering the country.

I didn't think through what the next few weeks or months would be like. I convinced myself that I could cope with anything England threw at me. It started as soon as I stood at the Customs and Immigration line at Heathrow Airport. After looking at my passport and proof of scholarship, a very blunt officer asked if I carried any health certificate. I stared at her in amazement. I had no idea what she was talking about. She explained that students from certain Third World countries with a documented history of infectious diseases were usually asked to present a certificate of good health. I had none, and as far as I could remember no one in the British Council or embassy in Yemen had suggested such a thing. That document, I later realized, could be vitally important for an international student in England. Because full-time students were eligible for National Health Service coverage, the idea was not to overload the system with sick students from poor countries. But back then, in the first few minutes of a new life in England, that encounter opened my eyes to the fact that, while I might be living in England, I would always be a Third World citizen suspected of having any number of infectious diseases.

I signed some kind of form and gave Faiza's address in Liverpool as a contact. Sure enough, within a week or two I had a visit from a health officer, who asked me to undergo some chest X-rays to eliminate any possibility of tuberculosis. "Don't take it personally," a very sensitive Faiza told me. I didn't, not because I was thick-skinned, but because I had too many distractions. I had newspapers and magazines to read, TV shows to watch, movies that were shown in their entirety, not edited by the censors like the ones we used to watch in Sana'a. This was the reason I wanted to study in England. I wanted to immerse myself in a culture that I perceived to be the exact opposite of my life in the Middle East.

But what I forgot to factor in was that although I'd arrived in England I hadn't exactly left Yemen behind. For economic and practical reasons, my sister's and aunt's homes in Liverpool initially served as shelter. By 1988 Faiza had been living there for seven years and my aunt for nearly fifteen. You wouldn't know it. Neither felt at home in her North England surroundings and did very little— nothing, in fact—to adapt to them.

My aunt Fatima, two years older than my mother, was barely educated and had lived much of her years in Liverpool a prisoner in her own home. She only went out with her husband, Ahmed

Sultan—my favourite family member at the time—or her one son, Nabil, who'd spent most of his adult life in Liverpool but longed to return to Aden. He arranged his own marriage to a woman from Aden he didn't know. I remember thinking that perhaps we could trade places. He could go back to Yemen and I'd take his British passport and settle in England.

The multicultural and predominantly Arabic and African Granby community, off Liverpool's crime- and riot-prone Princess Road, represented a kind of immigrant experience that I'd spend the rest of my life avoiding: closed-off households that showed no interest in British culture or civic society. My aunt, who passed away in November 2011, turned her house into a shrine to all things Yemeni. Ethnic food markets provided her with almost any ingredient she needed to prepare the same meals she made back in Aden, as well as khat. The living room was turned into a *diwan* for chewing khat and smoking hookah. It was difficult to tell if they adopted this way of life to preserve Yemeni roots or as a retreat from British society, which, while by no means welcoming of all immigrants, had served them well financially. The only sign they were living in England in that household in the 1980s was the TV, which was usually on, set on mute. By the time Arab satellite TV began carrying channels from all over the Middle East the following decade, the British programs were effectively obsolete.

Faiza fared a bit better in that department, but only a bit. She and her husband ran a popular corner store in Walton, a working-class but mainly white neighbourhood. The store was sandwiched between the football grounds of the city's two main teams, Liverpool and Everton, so it did well on game days. Faiza had to learn the art of chit-chatting with customers while bringing them their cigarettes, cat food or the morning paper. It must have been hard for her to go from being the daughter of a business tycoon in a British colony to a shopkeeper's wife in Britain, but she coped well. She was obsessed with Princess Diana and would go through all the tabloids looking for her pictures. The odd brat or yob would occasionally give her and her husband, Hamza, a hard time, but by and large the two enjoyed a good income and a quiet if not always happy married life. Faiza had not been able to conceive. That part of their lives only got more problematic later in their marriage, but in those early years the issue of children didn't define their world.

Once the store was closed, she and her husband would go upstairs to their flat and spend the evening watching videos of Egyptian films and the odd British program. Faiza rarely went out at night, and visits to the shopping centre and back during the day became her only leisure activity. As soon as I arrived, I did some research for her to find the closest schools offering courses in English as second language so she could improve her spoken and written English. At the very least she could watch TV without asking me to translate anything more complicated than chat-show banter. She declined. Too old for school, she said. Our mother responded the same way when Mohamed and her older daughters suggested she learn how to read and write when we lived in Beirut. In retrospect, perhaps Faiza didn't want to come across as better educated than her husband, himself a high-school dropout who worked as a sailor for many years before settling in Liverpool. I understood about half of what he said. He spoke a strange mix of Arabic and English that suggested both were his second language.

My Liverpool family's England would not be mine. I didn't see the point of living somewhere that could be sliced off and transported back to Yemen without any noticeable difference. I completely understand the current European (and even North American) hostility to multiculturalism and the several declarations of its failure by the likes of Angela Merkel, Germany's chancellor. The Arab community was still a relatively new one in Britain despite the long colonial history that bound people from the Middle East and Arabian Gulf with the monarchy. Still, the way it isolated itself from the general British experience and the hostile tone with which, for example, my aunt and sister talked about the decadent English folks with whom they did daily business struck me as inexplicable. They often cited the evidence of knocked-up teenagers as proof of a lack of morals in British society. Why, I wondered, couldn't they appreciate the freedoms of that society instead? How could they still long for a life in Yemen and talk fondly of family and friends back home who had no right to express themselves?

To me, it all came down to the issue of gender and sexual freedom. I was finally free to walk into a gay bar without looking over my shoulder or fear of getting arrested. Even when I became familiar with the notion of gay bashing—particularly in the more violent north of England—I still figured it was better to experience homophobia from some drunken yobs than from an organized state or as part of religious crackdown. I knew immediately that what I'd gained by moving to England outweighed what I'd lost by moving away from the Arab world.

Still, it took me a year to break away from the influence of family in Liverpool. As I settled into the Keele University campus, I made fewer trips back to Liverpool. Slowly, I began to feel uncomfortable speaking Arabic. I was convinced that the more I spoke it, the less my chance of reaching native-level English proficiency. From here on, Arabic would be on an as-needed basis. I had stopped listening to Arabic music many years before, so I now graduated to the next level of cultural abandonment. I would not cook with the spices that Faiza loaded into my luggage when she and Hamza drove me to the Keele campus. For one thing, the communal kitchen in our student residence was too small, and I felt self-conscious about the aroma in such tight quarters. Instead, I bought a lot of ready-made meals at a supermarket—the kind that was an adventure for me in Cairo only a few years before.

One of the first things I noticed about this change of diet, however, was a constant stomach cramp and gas. For over twenty years I'd seldom eaten anything that hadn't been prepared in the family kitchen from scratch, and suddenly eating all this pre-packaged food wreaked havoc on my system. The general practitioner I went to see on campus suggested I learn to cook more fresh food. I blurted out that I came from a culture where men didn't cook. "Well, you're not there anymore," he quietly responded. Partly out of laziness and partly because of a longing to immerse myself in British culture, I associated Arabic food with the kind of life that my sister and aunt were leading in Liverpool.

I guess all of that would suggest I was self-loathing. I think I was. I wanted to be as English as possible. I listened carefully to classmates and professors and made notes of expressions and rhythms of speech that sounded distinctly British. I remember a police officer—as a foreign student I had to register with the Home Office—telling me to get in touch if I was ever "in a spot of bother." What a great expression, and in it went into my mental database. I had a very solid English education in Cairo, but nothing compared to this opportunity to live the language—a language that I associated not just with survival but with my right to live in dignity as a gay man.

Of course, that dream of living the language, and my impulse to idealize English language and literature, would be interrupted every time I encountered some form of racism or discrimination. I rationalized it to myself by remembering the harassment and humiliation I experienced at the hands of the Yemeni internal security men when I first moved to Sana'a. If people from my own country did that to me, I could at least survive this occasional outburst of verbal violence. I got called Paki several times, even on campus. Sometimes the encounters scared me so much I'd walk as fast as I could and hail the first cab I found. My trusty British Council guidebook told me to ignore these jeers, as it was best not to engage the people who made such comments in a conversation or a fight. Luckily, I developed a thicker skin, but for the rest of my time in England, my comfort level in that country would be undercut by its racial violence. I learned to avoid being out late at night or on weekends. I avoided pubs, as I soon realized that most of these incidents happened at closing time and involved people who'd had one-too-many pints. I never told my mother or any of my siblings about these early experiences. It was in my best interest to cultivate a blemish-free image of life in England in order not to give them any excuse to ask me to return to Yemen.

Faiza called several times a week to check in on me. When it became evident that she wouldn't be able to have children of her own, she continued instead in her old role as my second mother. I felt awkward standing in a corridor in the hall of residence, talking on a pay phone in Arabic as students came and went. Other international students would talk freely to friends and family in Greek, Cantonese or Spanish, but I resented those few minutes every other day that took me away from English and transported me back to conversations about gossip and feuds in the Yemeni community in Liverpool—or just news about Yemen itself. After a year of living in Keele, I thought less and less of my parents and siblings. They became symbols of repression, even as I understood that the women were more victims than oppressors. What struck me about that first year in England was how my life constantly changed while theirs remained static. It was a given that mine would change. But theirs seemed to be particularly resistant to new developments. Changing jobs was about as radical as it got, and even that happened too rarely. My mother and father continued to ignore each other, while my sisters kept giving up their freedoms by integrating more into Sana'a society. I began to sense the widening gap between us just by talking on the phone. Their language and way of life were that of the Quran, a world of religious observance and intolerance, in my opinion. "What have we done to you?" my brother-in-law Hamza would often ask me on the phone when I turned down an invitation to go to Liverpool for the weekend or to celebrate eids, the Muslim feasts. I used work as an excuse—although it was a genuine one.

STUDYING ENGLISH LITERATURE in England was harder than I thought. In Cairo I was a star student, even though I spent most of my college time fooling around in the underground gay scene and used classes and "library time" as excuses to get out of the house, particularly when one of my parents was visiting from Sana'a. At Keele, however, and specially once I passed to the master's level, I found the critical theory of studying literature to be challenging. All I wanted was to learn English so I could escape my Arabic roots. All that stuff about deconstruction and psychoanalysis didn't interest me. I preferred history and historiography to illuminate the literary texts. While that was still possible to do at an undergraduate level, the M.A. course I chose didn't always accommodate that approach. Thinking that I just needed to avoid any program with poetry courses, I'd picked one in twentieth-century British fiction. But I hadn't really thought about how modernism changed the way fiction was written and analyzed. As long as I was reading the realists (H.G. Wells, Arnold Bennett, John Galsworthy), I was doing just fine. Bring in James Joyce or Virginia Woolf and I'd be lost. I couldn't concentrate on narratives without strong plot lines and with too much interior monologue.

I couldn't concentrate in general, as I began to be distracted by the possibilities of the gay scene in Stoke-on-Trent, where I later moved and rented a room in a house with a gay landlord, Tony. I just couldn't get enough of talking to Tony about all things gay and filling in the gaps in my sexual education. Tony, a sweet and ambitious young solicitor, obliged. His stories of dancing in clubs, meeting other men and having a string of one-night stands kept me awake until the early hours of the morning. Who needed to study boring old literature when Staffordshire could be such a seedy little fantasy. I'd count the days until Saturday—and when I couldn't wait, Friday—to go with Tony to the local club in Henley, one of the "five towns" that made up Stoke-on-Trent. I'd been to gay bars in London but never until then to a dance club. The idea of men dancing together was so life-affirming, so utterly different from anything I'd experienced before. Even if, with my nerdy glasses and conservative clothing, I didn't get to dance or meet that many people on the first few visits, I was thrilled to be in that environment. Occasionally, I'd stop and ask myself, What would my family say if they saw me now? And what would that army captain in Sana'a who'd tell me to toughen up and act like a man make of all this? But the loud music and the crowded bar distracted me from any serious comparative cultural analysis.

Then I met Raymond, my first romance. A previously married older gentleman—he'd be my age now, late forties—whose smile and gentle embrace confirmed that I'd made the right choice in life. But I had no reference for an emotional life with another man. All I knew was sex. I didn't know what was required of me to be, and keep, a boyfriend. No doubt that was the cumulative effect of more than two decades of homophobia in the Arab world and the complete absence of any discussion of emotions when you're a man. Raymond couldn't understand why I felt uncomfortable holding hands even in a dark movie theatre. I could enjoy the sex and the gay identity but not the emotional life and responsibility that came with it. It would be six years of life in England before I connected all these strands.

A string of flings and one-night stands later, I felt right at home as a sexually active gay man. The thought of losing that and being forced back to Yemen once I completed my M.A. terrified me. I'd be going back to a place where what I'd been doing in the last two years was punishable by public lashings. I'd be back in the company of Helmi, who would ask why I refused to pray five times a day. I would no longer feel uncomfortable being who I was. My emotional home was in the West, even if my ancestral one was elsewhere on the map.

A RETURN TO YEMEN was out of the question for more than just personal reasons. When Saddam Hussein invaded Kuwait in the summer of 1990, he may have changed the course of history in the region, but he also plunged Yemen into a social and economic crisis from which it never recovered. Indeed, I trace the political and financial downfall of Yemen to that summer. While the rest of the world condemned the invasion, Yemen and Cuba endorsed it. Yemen's President Saleh was largely regarded as Saddam's sidekick. Whatever Saddam wanted, Saleh got for him. But this latest gesture of support would prove too costly, because soon thereafter most of the Gulf Arab states, which sided with Kuwait, punished the expatriate Yemeni communities in their lands by terminating work contracts for the more professional class of immigrants and immediately expelling hundreds of thousands of low-paid and temporary Yemeni workers.

Alongside Egyptians, Filipinos and other people from South Asia, Yemenis had worked as cheap labour in such countries as

Saudi Arabia, Bahrain, the United Arab Emirates (UAE) and Qatar. Now, without warning, Sana'a was flooded with returning workers from the Gulf states. Some went straight to their native villages or small towns, but the majority settled in Sana'a since it was the capital and economic centre of the country. A sparsely populated city that could barely accommodate its own citizens in terms of social and medical services before August 1990 cracked under the pressure of this new wave of reverse migration. Economically, Yemen lost the revenue it earned when these workers—especially the single male emigrants—remitted their earnings to their families. Inflation began to undercut the purchasing power of the local population. The US dollar, worth about twenty riyals at the start of the summer, stood at forty or sixty, and then kept jumping by ten riyals every few months. The higher it got, the lower the standard of living became for the average Yemeni, and salaries were frozen to help pay for the influx of returning citizens.

The returning Yemenis came in with different sets of social and religious norms. Those who moved back from the more tolerant (relatively speaking) nations of Qatar or UAE largely followed the same moderate form of Islam they were exposed to over there. But the much larger group of migrants from Saudi Arabia brought back the harsher traditions of Wahhabism, which made Yemeni society suddenly even more intolerant towards women and possibly a little bit dangerous as well. Not that Yemen would ever be considered a role model for women's rights, but compared to Saudi Arabia it probably should be. In their phone calls and letters to me, my sisters mentioned harassment in the souks and shopping centres from groups of men who frowned on women driving cars or going out without male companions. I felt terrible for my sisters, who were getting increasingly trapped in a Yemen that no longer even offered them the same financial rewards as before.

I had to plot an exit into North America or Australia or find a way to stay in Britain a little while longer. I guessed a Ph.D. in English would at least give me five more years of borrowed time. I dreaded telling my mother what I was planning, but when I called her to break the news later that summer, her response captured the sudden change in Yemen. "What's your hurry. There's nothing to come back to." I sat in my Stoke-on-Trent living room shortly after that call and mulled over her reaction. By then I'd thought that Safia would want me back so badly she'd more or less order my return. She was the one who told me to run away, and now her advice was to keep running. Saddam may have invaded Kuwait, but he'd destroyed what little hope Yemenis had for their future.

Like my father before me, but without the family weight he carried on his shoulders, I needed to find new shelter.

THE LAST THING I WANTED to do was study for five more years. Although I did well in my master's dissertation and enjoyed working on the fantasias of local Staffordshire author Arnold Bennett, a career as an academic would take me away from having fun. I hated sitting in a classroom and didn't enjoy discussions with my professors, mainly because I barely had time to finish the novels we were supposed to read. I felt better when I realized that the English doctoral system was a leftover from the old Oxbridge days. A Ph.D. candidate got a supervisor and a library card and was left alone. The system was developed to make a scholar out of a doctoral student—unlike the North American model, which encourages general knowledge and teaching skills. In that case, I could choose a pre-modern period to focus on and develop a thesis that worked within my area of strength: literary history. When additional funding came through from the British Council, I tried to get into any college in the University of London so I could be at the centre of its gay life. I know how disappointing this must be to my colleagues and students who hold my academic achievements in high regard. In my case, academia was an acquired taste. To be on the safe side, I also applied to Nottingham University, since an old English friend from the days of the Nile Hilton Tavern relocated there and I had visited him in the past. Its English department is still one of the best in the country, and its then-chair, Norman Page, was a renowned Victorian specialist. I had made up my mind to focus on the novels of Wilkie Collins for what started out as sentimental reasons.

While living in Sana'a, I'd stumbled upon a second-hand copy of *The Moonstone* that someone donated to the British Council. The back-cover blurb suggested a narrative that was both English with hints of colonial intrigue—Indian jewels, curses and so on. *The Woman in White,* an earlier novel by Collins, had become one of my all-time favourite books when I read it a few months before. It's hard to explain the appeal of Victorian mystery novels for a Yemeni man in Sana'a, but I was hooked. If I had to do a Ph.D. in English, then I'd better focus on something I knew I enjoyed. The more English it was, the better. Part of my wilful suppression of my Arabic identity meant avoiding obvious choices for an Arab scholar: travel literature set in the Middle East or translations by Sir Richard Burton (*The Arabian Nights*). I didn't want a Ph.D. that relied on my Arabic knowledge. I wished that part of my life negated, made irrelevant. I botched my interview at Birkbeck College in the University of London by showing up underprepared. I had spent the night before watching a drag show at the Vauxhall Tavern in South London. When I received a firm offer from Nottingham University—and the expected rejection from Birkbeck—I made the move in the fall of 1990.

Any hope of staying away emotionally and politically from the Arab world was dashed a few months later when the first Gulf War erupted in January 1991, five months after Saddam invaded Kuwait. Yemen's condemnation of the American-led bombing of Iraq further isolated it from the world and identified it as an unfriendly state. (Its status as a terror-supporting country was yet to come, but the seeds were planted then.) I'd gone from being the child of a British colony to a person of interest based on my passport, no more than a piece of paper as far as I was concerned. Day-to-day living in Nottingham was unaffected by the war, but when later that summer I wanted to visit the United States for a vacation—it'd been my dream for more than a decade to set foot in New York and San Francisco—I knew that holding a Yemeni passport would forever mean being interrogated at visa offices and airports around the world. Even with a Canadian passport now, I still have an irrational fear of crossing international borders. Someone will come and drag me away, transport me back to Yemen and I'll lose everything I have. It happened to Maher Arar, didn't it? I don't think that fear ever goes away if you're a man of Arab origin.

Still, I managed to get an American visa after submitting a letter of support from the British Council and, to my surprise and relief, made it through US Customs in Boston in the summer of 1991 with nothing more than the standard questions about my last visit to the Middle East and the purpose of my visit to the US. I had a thirty-day ticket for unlimited standby travel anywhere Delta Airlines flew within the continental USA and that convinced the immigration officer that I was a legitimate tourist. Five years earlier I had sat in my room in Sana'a fantasizing about what it would be like to fly from New York to LA. Now I was about to experience it. I wanted to visit every city I'd read about in magazines or seen in movies growing up in Cairo. I visited my Egyptian friend Nancy in her new home in Chicago because it was a city I'd heard mentioned so many times. I stopped in New Orleans, since I'd read some literature of the Deep South as a student in Cairo. And in Dallas, because I knew that was where JFK was assassinated. And as far as I was concerned, a trip to San Francisco and a walk through the Castro—a street I first read about in 1983 in an article about AIDS—was the most important item on my itinerary, followed closely by a stop in New York City.

I had never set foot in New York before, but I knew it so well. One of my favourite films as a teen was *An Unmarried Woman,* starring Jill Clayburgh and Alan Bates, who I thought back then was the sexiest man alive, as her bearded British artist boyfriend. To me, the film's message of freedom—which my then newly divorced sister Fathia also appreciated—and the New York landscape were inseparable.

As terrified as I was to be alone in NYC (and in a youth hostel), experiencing the thrill of being in a Broadway theatre (Neil Simon's *Lost in Yonkers,* starring a relatively unknown Kevin Spacey, was my first show) and actually walking up and down Christopher Street became my pilgrimage. Although I thought the gay bars on Christopher Street were seedy and the people ugly, I felt that I had to find a way to move to the West. I just didn't know how it could be done, and with the Gulf War and Yemen's troublemaking reputation, my chances were getting slimmer.

Back in England, I continued to live as much of an Arabic-free life as I could. Even when talking to another Ph.D. student from Bahrain, I'd use English. The only Arabic I spoke was on my increasingly rare visits to Liverpool and rarer calls home. But I knew this couldn't continue, as I was long overdue for a family visit to Yemen, my first in over four years. It'd be my first encounter with the post-Kuwait Sana'a and a test of my relationship with my family, from whom I had drifted emotionally in the intervening years. The trip also meant going back into the closet and avoiding any questions about my personal life, including the obvious one: When are you getting married? I didn't really want to spend time with my father and be reminded of the fact that since he'd moved us to Yemen, he had made no money whatsoever. But in the spring of 1992, I forced myself to go home, mainly to see my mother.

CHAPTER NINE

SANA'A

Return

So much had changed in four years in Sana'a. Cars with Saudi licence plates clogged its once-deserted side streets. New buildings erupted in places where green patches once provided some relief from the concrete, leaving the local architecture little breathing room. If there was an inch of land for sale, some developer with money from his Gulf years bought it to build a low-rise or a family home.

At Sana'a International Airport, Wahbi and Khairy greeted me. Both looked much older than their thirty-two and thirty years, respectively. But that was to be expected. The heat and chewing khat can do damage to the skin, since both are dehydrating. As we drove from the airport to our new family home in the Zubieri district of Sana'a, I looked at the streets and passersby with disbelief. Nine months earlier I was knocking back beers in New York City's gay bars. That felt more natural and at home to me than being in a car in Sana'a with my own brothers. Even after living there and recognizing its quaintness, I still felt like a stranger in Sana'a. And now, on top of it all, I had no choice but to speak in Arabic for three weeks.

At home I rushed to kiss my mother, whose arthritis had got so severe she was now completely housebound, except for visits to the doctors. My sisters greeted me with warmth and affection, but I saw the haggard look on their faces. Since the return of approximately one million migrants to Yemen, everything in Sana'a had turned into a struggle, from finding a new job to commuting to work if you had one. So far, my three sisters who lived at home—Ferial, Hoda and Raja'a—were still employed, but the higher cost of living and stagnant salaries left them with little disposable income. Holidays in Cairo, which were once as easy as stopping at the travel agent and packing a bag, became huge investments. They felt not just psychologically trapped in Yemen, but physically, too.

And there was my father. Almost a decade after relocating the family to its ancestral home he was still without meaningful income or any chance of resuming that thriving career as a real-estate developer. His world consisted of watching the news on TV and whiling away the time playing with his grandchildren. At sixty-seven he, too, looked much older. Thinner as well. We didn't know it then, but the cancer that killed him three years later had probably begun to invade his body. For the first time in my adult life, he replied in Arabic every time I started a conversation in English. I knew that in the past he took any opportunity to practise his English, so I often volunteered to keep him talking. Not now. His English was fading, and while I associated the language with my liberation, he linked it with his long-gone glory days. From here on, it had to be Arabic for this former anglophile.

As much as I felt for my parents, my main concern was for my sisters. It was their life, and if religion pleased them, then so be it. But to me it looked like their faith was a refuge, a necessity, and not an intellectual choice. Still, there was a spark in them and a desire to find out about my life (and Faiza's) in England. The same didn't apply to my brothers, who had begun to see the West as being synonymous with the oppression of Muslims in Iraq and Afghanistan and, later, Eastern Europe. If my sisters were curious, my brothers were confrontational. I may have been successfully working towards a doctorate in English—in itself a major academic achievement no matter what my motivations were—but my brothers saw me as someone who'd betrayed his heritage and was brainwashed by the permissive West. We once lived in a world where East and West overlapped, where liking Western music didn't suggest a cultural betrayal but merely a preference. The dividing lines between Eastern and Western cultures were firmly in place now. The attitude would soften considerably when Bill Clinton took office later that year, but the divisive legacy of the first Gulf War in political and social terms in Yemen couldn't be underestimated.

If I had any lingering doubts regarding Yemen, that trip took care of them. My path in life couldn't just be different from my own flesh and blood; I needed to be free of the legacy of guilt and abandonment I felt when visiting them. Back in England, I convinced myself to keep my distance from them. Their suffering forced me to examine a life that I didn't want for myself, and I could do nothing to change it for them. I don't know when and how I became so heartless and selfish. Family members drift apart and reconcile all the time, and certainly events of 2011 made me sick with worry about their safety and well-being. But back then, as my sisters' embrace of Islam and their integration into Yemeni society became more complete, I saw no point in having this family as a compass for my life. History hasn't helped, and larger ideological shifts made the gulf even bigger.

The next came two years later, in 1994, when a civil war broke out between the formerly communist South and the pro-capital North Yemen—the two having been united in a shotgun wedding in 1990 to avoid fighting over oil and gas revenues. My family had coped with all kinds of turmoil in the Arab world: a nationalist revolution in Aden, sectarian acts of violence in Beirut and fundamentalism and political assassinations in Cairo. But this was their first taste of a civil war—although not the last, as events in 2011 proved. Forces in the southern faction targeted Sana'a with missiles, which initially fell well outside our neighbourhood. In the days before the internet, I followed the news on TV and in newspapers with a sense of despair. I had nightmares about my mother being trapped at home while my siblings and father ran away to escape the rockets falling on our neighbourhood. Which, as I was told later, wasn't that far from what they had to do, but without leaving Safia behind. The last thing that country needed was a civil war. Whatever infrastructure it had was being devastated, and no one was quite sure how its cities could be rebuilt.

Since I was living at the time in a graduate hall of residence at Nottingham University with one pay phone for eighteen students, it made more sense for me to spend some time with Faiza in Liverpool. This way we could call Sana'a every day to make sure no one was hurt in the war. That visit brought home the difference between Faiza and me. My sister was devastated by the news coming from Yemen; I, on the other hand, was determined to use this war as an excuse never to return to that country again. I knew that my relationship with my mother would be the one serious hitch in my plans. Even as I kept repeating her words in my head—"escape," "there's nothing to come back to"—I knew that she was secretly hoping I'd come home and keep her company. A few weeks later, a truce was called and normal life of sorts resumed in Yemen. But I had already made up my mind not to go back even for a visit.

I was now in a relationship with my first real partner, a German doctor in London called Jochem, and my circle of friends in Nottingham and elsewhere in England expanded. Staying on in England would be a difficult task, as it'd been more than twenty-five years since my father had given up our British passports. (The taxation rate for British nationals during the 1970s would have eaten into the income he relied on to raise his eleven children.) The paperwork involved to reclaim my British citizenship was too complicated, and the whole process could take years without any guarantee of success. I wasn't really keen on staying in England, anyway. I had visited the United States again in the summer of 1993 and fallen in love with its more egalitarian spirit. I pictured myself living in Seattle or San Francisco. I'd got what I wanted out of England: the education and the time to plan my next move.

IF I WERE TO FIND a new home, it would have to be after finishing my Ph.D., and it would have to be in the New World: either the United States or Canada, or Australia or New Zealand. I focused all my energy on the latter two, borrowing money from my sister to hire an immigration consultant for New Zealand, which seemed the most likely choice. But just like in that adage "Life is what happens when you're busy making other plans," Canada moved to the top of my list by pure chance.

I had arranged to meet up with my good friend Jago, a fellow Ph.D. student and now a professor at London's Brunel University. We were to have lunch together on campus, but he called to say he'd be late. Since I was already dressed, I made my way to the café where we'd arranged to meet. I had time to spare, so I stopped by an employment and recruitment fair aimed at undergraduates. A poster for an agency that specialized in immigration to Canada caught my eye. It was the only immigration booth in the fair. The man working the booth asked me a few questions (age, education, work experience) and said that based on what I'd just told him I'd be a good candidate for immigration—so much so that he suggested I go it alone and apply directly to the Canadian Consular Services in London, skipping the middleman (himself). I wonder if this nice man, whose name I don't think I caught, knows how he changed my life in that one brief encounter. Canada? What did I know about Canada except for Anne Murray and possibly *The Kids in the Hall,* then running on Channel 4? I must admit that I knew Murray very well. I discovered her music in Cairo in 1983 at a quaint little music shop in my old high-school neighbourhood of Zamalek. It was a "very best" compilation that charted her career from "Snowbird" until about 1982. Something about her gravelly voice and laidback melodies struck a chord with me. I don't think I knew she was Canadian back then, and I don't even think I had any associations with Canada. But a decade later in Nottingham, it seemed like Murray's home country could be mine.

In those primitive, pre-internet days, I went to the library and flipped to "Canada" in the card index. My friend Liz was finishing a degree in American studies and suggested I look up a magazine called *Maclean's* to get an idea of what life there was like. She knew it because her mother was a Canadian who had moved to England in the 1940s but kept up with her family in Ottawa. And next time I found myself in London, Liz suggested, I should also check out a paper called the *Globe and Mail.* I had never heard of that, either. I didn't even know where in Canada I might settle, assuming I got a landed-immigrant visa. Weather-wise, British Columbia made the most sense. In 1993, as part of my Ph.D., I'd attended an academic conference in Santa Cruz, California, and travelled up to Seattle, a city I'd previously visited in 1991 and loved instantly. In Seattle I met a friendly gay couple from Vancouver who had come down for the weekend, and they mentioned how their province of British Columbia boasted the mildest weather. That was about all the thinking I did on the subject of where to settle. At the very least I could also weekend in Seattle whenever I wanted to.

I completed the detailed application, sent a certified cheque to the receiver general and waited to hear from the Canadian Consular Services. After about three months, I received notification to show up for an interview in London in July 1995. I was nervous about it for weeks, but the actual interview felt more like a coffee chat. The officer in charge of my application suggested Toronto might be a better place than Vancouver. I had worked with my Ph.D. supervisor on scholarly and popular editions of Victorian novels, including a collection of short stories by Wilkie Collins, and so my most relevant work experience was in publishing. For that kind of work, he said, I should be in Toronto.

Toronto? I had vague recollections of reading some travel stories about the city in the weekend papers. The word "dull" always crept into the copy. I always mixed it up in my mind with Ottawa. But it was in North America, and the guidebooks I consulted in the library informed me that it was a largely liberal and gay-friendly destination. While I qualified in the points system that managed professional immigration to Canada, and passed the medical tests, a security clearance would prove more difficult. The same immigration officer asked me to be patient, as my place of birth, of course, was often treated suspiciously in applications. I waited and waited.

IT WAS JUST AS WELL that I couldn't get the final approval as fast as I had hoped. My mind was preoccupied with a visit from my father, who had travelled to Liverpool in the hope of stopping the lung cancer from spreading. Khairy accompanied him, as Mohamed was too frail to travel alone. His visit marked the first and only time Mohamed and I were in England at the same time. A part of the Yemen that I'd tried to avoid for so many years had followed me to England.

It was a trying time, and not just because of the cancer. Mohamed's England existed only in his memories, and this was his first visit to his daughter's home in Liverpool since she got married in 1981. She lived in a working-class neighbourhood above the corner shop where she and her husband worked seven days a week. Mohamed had heard stories of her life and definitely knew she wasn't living in Mayfair, but he still couldn't adjust to seeing his daughter serving customers from behind the counter. Wasn't she just like the people who'd rented his storefronts in Aden?

Although he was almost sixty-nine, he still showed traces of the old gentleman. He packed a large suitcase with several business suits, ties and more cufflinks than you'd see in a small menswear store. He didn't forget the comb he always carried in the inside pocket of his jacket even when he had little hair left. All that was charming and, to my brother and sister and me, a distraction from the fact that his lung cancer had metastasized.

The doctors in the private hospital where we placed Mohamed had given him just a few weeks to live, a piece of news they didn't tell him. For some reason, his doctor thought he wouldn't be able to handle the news. Some patients, the doctor said, were better off not knowing. He called that one right. Mohamed refused to acknowledge that he even had cancer. When the doctors prescribed him morphine to alleviate the pain of chemotherapy, he voiced his concerns about its addictive nature. I strongly believe that he didn't think he should die. Not when the second chapter of his life—the one that began in 1967 when we left Aden—had been such a failure. He still dreamed of that comeback, that return to his old glory. So much so that he never made a will, even when his own brother urged him to write one before he left for England.

In the hospital and at my sister's home, this visit gave me a chance to talk to Mohamed more about the decisions he made in life, raising a large family that he'd moved around so much. His visit coincided with the fiftieth anniversary of VE day, and we watched the live celebrations on TV as he talked about his England of the 1940s, repeating the same stories that we grew up listening to. It was during those conversations that I learned how much he was in love with my mother and how their estrangement for the better part of the previous decade had depressed him almost as much as losing his property. He couldn't understand how she'd turned her back on him after all he'd done for her. He thought she was ungrateful for resenting the fact he that lived off the income his children brought into the house. Hadn't he shouldered the responsibility for her and all the children—and a host of relatives—for the previous four decades?

When it came to my life, he acknowledged that he was upset that I had distanced myself so much from my own family, language and culture. He said I had started acting selfishly ever since my first trip to England in 1984. "There'll come a time when you'll realize that your place is at home with your brothers and sisters," he added. When I told him about my plan to immigrate to Canada, his reaction was instant. "This would devastate your mother." He then went to sleep, his way of cutting the conversation short. So much for saying goodbyes and finding closure. While I knew he was proud of my achievements, to him I'd failed the one important test in life: sticking with your own family. In his estimation Faiza offered a better model, as she went home every year, called regularly and didn't struggle speaking Arabic like I did.

I cried uncontrollably for the first time in my life on the last morning I saw him in Liverpool. Once he realized that there was nothing that England and its doctors could do to save his life, he decided he wanted to die in Yemen. I hired a minivan and driver for Gatwick Airport, put him, Khairy and Faiza in it, kissed them and waved goodbye. He died in August of that year, just six weeks short of his seventieth birthday.

AFTER RETURNING TO NOTTINGHAM to complete my Ph.D. thesis, which I had put on hold for six weeks during Mohamed's visit, I resumed my periodic calls to the Canadian Consular Services to check in on the status of the application. I wish I could remember his name, but the same officer who interviewed me and had been handling my case told me to hang up and call back in a couple of hours. I didn't know what to expect. When I did call back, he had wrestled my security clearance from wherever he had to. My immigration papers would be in the post in a few weeks. "Welcome to Canada," he said and ended the call.

Early in December 1995, a brown envelope arrived in the communal mailbox of the graduate apartment building where I had been living for more than four years. It was nondescript and came with the regular delivery. It could easily have got lost in the Christmas rush. It contained that piece of paper I'd been dreaming of and chasing for many years: my right to claim residency in a Western democracy, as far away from Yemen and my family as possible. I rushed upstairs to my third-floor apartment, waited until the cleaning lady had left and sat alone in the kitchen, reading and re-reading the document and a one-page sheet of instructions about what to do when you first landed at a Canadian port of entry. I was still at least a couple of weeks away from wrapping up my thesis, but I could hardly concentrate on the copyediting and revisions that I was expected to complete before handing it to my internal and external examiners. Somehow it didn't even matter if I passed or not. The whole point of doing the thesis was to get that piece of paper. I calmed down after a few days and knew I'd do better in Canada with a completed Ph.D. under my belt—which I had by April 1996, after revisions to my thesis that included adding a new chapter. My mind was on Canada, but until I finished that last chapter, part of it had to stay in Victorian England. I received the final approval for my thesis on April 13 or 14, booked a one-way ticket to Toronto around the same week, and was aboard a British Airways flight on April 20. A Saturday, since two friends insisted on driving me to Heathrow on their day off work. I had bought a travel guide in a bookstore in London, which I never really looked at until I was on that flight.

I didn't tell my family, who were expecting me back in Yemen that spring, until the last minute. They had no frame of reference for Canada aside from another of my father's many failed projects, which involved a Canadian company that sold wheat silos. I remember my sister Hoda telling me, somewhat sternly, that I had to break the news to my mother. Safia had been counting the days until she'd see me again. I just couldn't tell her the whole truth at once, so I said I was going to live there for a few years to get more work experience. She probably saw through the lie but said nothing. Faiza took it badly, as my presence in England had given her some kind of family anchor outside a (beyond doubt now) childless marriage.

Worst of all, I had to break up a loving relationship with Jochem. It had taken almost ten years before I found someone to love me and to love. And now I had no choice but to leave him behind. My desire to move to the West legally and not just on a student visa outweighed all these disappointments and heartbreaks. By now I was also used to leading with my mind. I couldn't afford to let my heart decide for me.

CHAPTER TEN

TORONTO

Home

As I settled into my seat on the flight from London to Toronto, I was terrified but arrogantly optimistic. I was now putting two continents and an ocean between me and my family and heritage. That should be enough physical and emotional distance. If Toronto lived up to the guidebook copy, I'd create a new family and traditions for myself. It was a lot to ask of a city (and a country) I'd never set foot in. My friend Liz from Nottingham University—the one who suggested I check out the *Globe and Mail* and *Maclean's*—had moved there a few months before my arrival and was my only contact.

I fell in love with Toronto instantly. Once I cleared Immigration, the nice officer actually said, "Welcome to Canada." I felt that I was indeed welcomed to this city. No one asked me if I had a history of infectious diseases. That was taken care of in the medical tests I'd done in Nottingham as part of my visa application. The first ride on the Toronto subway on my second day was a revelation. I was accustomed to being the only person of colour on the buses in Nottingham or in certain parts of Liverpool. Now, to be surrounded by so many people who spoke different languages and came from almost every part of the globe instantly laid to rest any self-consciousness I might have had about being the FOB—fresh-off-the-boat—immigrant. Even after eight years of absorbing local life in England, I still felt like an outsider.

In less than ten days in Toronto I was sharing an apartment with a gay man and a straight woman in the Little Italy neighbour-hood of the city, which looked both refined and bohemian, just like one of those exterior shots in the American sitcoms I'd watched for years in Cairo and in England. The clincher for me was the stop a mere five-minute walk from my new home on Markham Street for the Wellesley bus, Number 94, which took me directly to Toronto's gay village at Church and Wellesley. None of this would strike read-ers who have lived in Toronto or other Western democracies as anything special. But after Cairo and Sana'a, where I lived a furtive and then closeted life, and despite the time in England, that bus ride had all the significance of a moon landing. A transportive experience, literally.

In Nottingham, the gay scene was mainly a couple of bars and one nightclub, all of which got busy on weekends only. I was now living in a city that had a definable gay neighbourhood with book-shops, coffee houses and bars that were open during the day. I don't think I had been to a gay bar in daylight except for maybe once in London with my then-partner. Every time I visited London, how-ever, I felt like a tourist with time limits. But in Toronto I could finally slow down and enjoy this new world, which, from here on, I would have every right to call mine.

Toronto would be my playground, but I also needed to find some kind of long-term employment to afford living here. I qualified as a book editor under the occupation-demand list that determined my eligibility as an immigrant to Canada. There was almost nothing

advertised anywhere that called for an editor with a English graduate degree, or at least nothing that I was qualified for. The Catch-22
of the new immigrant's life: to get work in Canada, you must have
experience in Canada. And you can't get that experience if no one
hires you in the first place. I had enough money to live for, at most,
two months without a job. If I was still unemployed by the end of
June, I'd have to re-examine my plans and possibly move to a place
in Canada where there might be more work opportunities. I was
told that Alberta's or British Columbia's stronger economy might
be more suitable for me, since both had labour shortages. I could
work there until I got the Canadian experience that all employers
expected. But the idea of leaving a city that I loved so much and so
quickly gave me the incentive to try harder.

I lucked out when a friend of a friend passed the name of a
contact at a temping agency in downtown Toronto, Kelly Services,
which usually supplied offices and telemarketing agencies with temporary workers. My first paycheque came from a two-day stint as a
telemarketer for the Toronto Symphony Orchestra. I don't think I
sold a single subscription. When it became clear that I wasn't cut
out for phone sales, and since I didn't have any secretarial or computer experience, I qualified for low-skill filing and mail-sorting
jobs. I couldn't afford not to take on such work. Nightshifts at the
Royal Bank on Front Street? Sure. Stuffing flyers at the *Toronto Sun*
plant? Why not? It didn't really matter to me that none of these jobs
remotely called on my education or skills. All I wanted was to cover
the rent and have enough to pay my grocery bills. It wasn't every
month that I could afford both. My sister would send me more cash,
all the while suggesting that I should just leave Canada and go home
to Yemen, where my education would be valued and food and shelter taken care of. Our conversations had the exact opposite effect.
To go home was to admit defeat and to let the family make decisions

for me. Freedom with poverty meant more to me than money without personal choice. I saw things like "position" and "home comforts" as Middle Eastern values that could get in the way of this new life in Toronto if I let them. I asked Faiza to be patient and promised to pay back the money when I could.

Ironically, it took the Middle East to make my life in Toronto tolerable. In late August I spotted an ad in an alternative weekly for an exhibition coordinator job at an artist-run gallery cooperative, YYZ Artists' Outlet. A Canadian-Arab curator was organizing a festival of contemporary video and visual art from the Arab world and diaspora. Knowledge of Arabic language and culture would be an advantage, the ad copy went. The very things I'd turned my back on might help me land a six-month contract, which would provide some peace of mind. Coming up with $513 for rent plus about $100 for phone and hydro bills every month was proving a struggle. I'd lost weight, as I couldn't afford to eat well and the stress of unemployment was wearing me down. I was a mama's boy turned scholarship kid who'd never had to fend for himself before.

I had to get that gallery job. So what if I had to speak or read Arabic while in Canada? I still think I got that job because the two kind women who interviewed me sensed my desperation. I had no art administration experience, although I had just successfully completed an adult-education course in copyediting at Ryerson University and one of the gallery job's requirements was to compile and edit the exhibition catalogue. No immigrant or general success story would be complete without that one lucky break, and mine was that exhibition, titled . . . *east of here . . . (re)imagining the "orient."* It was heavy on post-colonialism and avant-garde video installations that I thought were too precious. (I much preferred the drag shows on Church Street for entertainment.) None of that mattered. The connections I made from that work experience opened up whole new worlds for me, from art administration to art writing, to alternative politics and independent culture. I soon discovered that while it was a struggle, you could live on very little in Toronto. Although that meant I couldn't even go out to the gay bars I craved so much on many weekends, I knew I could still go to the Second Cup at the corner of Church and Wellesley and stretch my five dollars over two cups of coffee.

When the contract was over, I had enough leads for part-time art gigs—curating a program on gay life in the Middle East for Inside Out, Toronto's queer film festival, or writing short art pieces for *Xtra!,* the city's gay biweekly. But I still needed a regular job that brought home at least a thousand dollars a month to cover food and shelter. I had never experienced winters like Toronto's, and buying suitable clothing was an expense I hadn't anticipated. My roommate's partner, Ben, donated some of his old coats and sweaters just to get me through my first Canadian winter. So back to the temping world I went, where I worked at an office in the Ministry of Education, filing and storing thousands of apprenticeship records. The contract kept getting extended, and I figured out a way to curry favour with the supervisors: don't act smart, and certainly not smarter than them. And whatever you do, I reminded myself, say nothing of the Ph.D. The building was on Church Street, which meant I could walk up and down through the gay village during my lunch or coffee breaks. It made going back to the cold archives almost bearable.

IN MY INFREQUENT LETTERS and phone calls to Yemen, I shared none of this with my family. To them, the move to Toronto would be considered a failure if I didn't have a house and, if I could drive, a car in the first year. People on both sides of the divide often talk of the Middle East as a spiritual destination and put down the West for its materialism, but my experience suggests otherwise. I could live well as a poor immigrant in Toronto because my life was enriched by many other things: from public libraries to public broadcasting to the many parks and free art galleries. And my roommate had a newspaper subscription, which meant free news before the internet made that the norm.

My mother, who initially thought that Canada was close to the United Kingdom, chided me for not flying to see my sister more often. (My aunt in Liverpool thought that Canada was next to Denmark when I first told her I'd be moving here.) Whenever they saw a news item about heavy snowfalls that even mentioned Canada, they'd call to make sure I was safe. At first I thought it was comic; after a while, I resented having to waste time telling them that snowstorms were part of everyday life here. I also started to call Yemen when I knew that my brothers wouldn't be home, since they'd ask me about the Arab community in Toronto. Where were the mosques? Had I met any good Muslim women I might consider for marriage? If not, they could make arrangements to ship one over for me. Just say the word.

I couldn't even explain to them that I had no interest in looking for Arab families in Canada to make me feel less homesick. I never got homesick. Sick from home, yes. Helmi and I got into a serious argument when he asked me to look after a friend of a friend who was seeking medical advice in Toronto. I didn't even know who he was, but the idea of spending days with someone visiting from Yemen seemed like such a waste of my time when I was still enraptured with Toronto's cultural and gay scene. Each call became an awkward reminder of the fact that the gap between me and them was widening, just as the gap between them and Yemen was tightening. There were few, if any, traces of the family I was born into and grew up with. That family was dead, killed off by a decade in Yemen.

I often wondered what would have happened to them (and me) had we not returned to Yemen. Would Cairo have protected our old family values? And if my father had managed the comeback he always dreamed of, would the financial security that came with it have shielded the family from the conservative influences of life in Sana'a? I don't have answers, but I do know that the Al-Solaylee family, like many others, got caught in a particular moment of history in the Middle East. They were always reacting to outside forces.

It was a perfect storm of so many political and social factors. The invasion of Afghanistan by the Soviet Union and the war that followed ushered in a new militarized form of Islamic resistance to foreign interference. The intifada in the Palestinian territories reminded many Muslims of the ongoing crisis there. The intifada in particular coincided with the penetration of round-the-clock Arabic-language news channels in the Middle East that trafficked in images of Palestinian rebellion and heroism in one news segment and victimization of the same people in the next. In Egypt, the newly visible Muslim Brotherhood's war against Anwar Sadat's peace treaty with Israel—and that country's widening gap between the rich and poor—created a society that tilted towards extremism. In Yemen, of course, the 1990 Iraqi invasion of Kuwait derailed all plans for economic prosperity and brought with it a wave of hardline Islamic followers returning from Saudi Arabia.

Day-to-day life in Yemen continued to reflect some of these larger geopolitical movements. Many members of al Qaeda in the Arabian Peninsula who operated out of Yemen were said to be graduates from the resistance to the Soviets in Afghanistan (as, of course, was the membership of the main organization). In 2000, members of al Qaeda in Yemen struck the navy destroyer USS *Cole* in the port of Aden, killing seventeen Americans. Ever since, Yemen struggled to achieve political stability within its own borders, which in turn drove away potential investors, who saw the country as too dangerous. Oil companies would do work with the devil, so they stayed in Yemen. Otherwise, its economic outlook was growing dim, and the social tensions increased. As did the dependence on religion. As Ferial once told me, she could escape it all whenever she read the Quran. It calmed her soul and gave her the strength to go on.

I, on the other hand, experienced something completely different. The longer I lived in Toronto, the more convinced I became that I'd made the right choice. And that's what it came down to. I had choices. I don't think my sisters, in particular, had any. Our lives diverged in so many ways, but the biggest difference was that I could make choices about every aspect of my life: where to live, how to live, what to spend my money on and who to sleep with.

Winters aside, everything about Toronto felt right, and I felt safe—just one among the millions of immigrants who over the decades have called this wonderful country home. "You are what this country is all about," an editor friend would remind me. I never lost faith in Canada, but I had to ask myself, why was I still underemployed? Did my very ethnic name and Middle Eastern background scare off employers? How much longer could I survive on minimum wage?

THE SUMMER OF 1997 was a turning point in my Canadian life. I found out about a very cheap one-bedroom apartment in Chinatown where the rent was even lower than what I paid for the house share. For $475 a month I had my own space in Toronto. It wasn't grand by any means. It sat in a cul-de-sac that you got to from an alleyway and backed on to the storeroom of a Chinese restaurant. But, again, the College streetcar took me to the edge of the gay village in ten minutes. My downstairs neighbour was a filmmaker and illustrator who also lived on very little. I became a regular contributor to *Xtra!* and applied for jobs at gay video stores and sex lines in order to make the most of my freedom. I didn't get any such jobs, but to place my byline in a gay paper fulfilled my dream of living openly. The odd Arab gay man I met at the time thought it was inappropriate and I should adopt a pen name. That defeated the purpose of coming to Canada, I felt.

Then I landed a three-month contract at an online agency that was about to put the content of a movie-listings magazine on a website. It was the heyday of the internet boom—a world of crazy ideas and no revenue models. The eccentric South African CEO who interviewed me for the job responded well to my immigrant story and hired me on the spot. Finally I had a job that would pay me about two thousand dollars a month, which to me was a fortune. I remember what I did with my first paycheque in late September: I went to the Bay and bought a TV and video recorder. I didn't have either in my first three months of living in my Chinatown apartment. I always tell my friends that I might be the only person in the world who missed out on the media frenzy surrounding the death and funeral of Princess Diana, as I followed it on the radio and in print only.

The three-month gig was extended to a regular contract with decent salary and health benefits. I needed the latter for the usual reasons: dental and drug plans. I also started writing for the urban magazine *Eye Weekly* (now the *Grid*) as a freelance arts and theatre reviewer. As much as I loved the gay ghetto, I wanted to get out of it as a journalist. It took almost two years, but the pieces of my new life in Canada had started to fall into place. I moved into a world of arts writing, gallery hopping and jazz and cabaret music, which became my forte in the gay press. I was now writing in the kind of magazines that I drooled over as a young man in Cairo and fought to bring into Yemen. It was a charmed life.

And it got more charming when I met my partner, Motaz, a York University dance student who was already performing in local festivals. He came from the same family as a famous Syrian poet that I'd read in school, and spoke English, French and Arabic. Beautiful. Crazy. Passionate. And six years younger. And while we may have shared an Arabic background, we looked like a mixed-race couple. He had light skin, light brown hair and green eyes. I didn't always like his work as a choreographer, but he became part of my new life as an arts writer in Toronto, and I a part of his dance world, especially once he moved back to Montreal after graduation.

I shared so little of my new life in Toronto with my family. They wouldn't have understood any part of it. And I wasn't sure which would be worse to them: that my partner was a man or that he was a choreographer-dancer. It was just another example of how the family I once knew was lost to me. In the Beirut or Cairo that we lived in, it was quite common to be surrounded by members of the creative community—writers, actors, journalists. We didn't just consume art but lived in a world that supported and encouraged it. But whenever I talked now to my sisters or brothers about my making a living writing about the arts, they'd encourage me to find something more respectable and stable. After a while I just started to tell them that I was working in a corporate job and that I made enough money to stop borrowing from my sister, whose own life changed radically in the fall of 1998.

Faiza's workaholic husband, Hamza, died at home from a heart attack while watching TV. It wasn't uncommon for him to fall asleep on the couch in their living room, but he'd always get up after midnight and go to bed. After all, he worked about twelve to fifteen hours a day, every day of the year, including Christmas. He loved Yemeni food that came drenched in fat, and never exercised. Whenever my sister, at the doctor's suggestion, tried to cook with olive oil or use less fat, Hamza would throw a temper tantrum. Food was his emotional release, in part because he didn't have a child to dote on. When Faiza woke up around 3 a.m. and noticed he wasn't there, she decided to check the living room. He was pronounced dead as soon as the paramedics arrived. I don't think Faiza was devastated on an emotional level. It was a loveless marriage, but she'd stayed in it because she got used to the routine of working in the shop and cooking a big meal that kept her husband from raising the issue of children. Now her main and immediate concern was to figure out what to do with the business, the house and her new life as a widow in England. A few days after Hamza's death, she called me for advice on banking and tax issues. I didn't have much to offer her.

If I had any lingering faith in family values or, for that matter, Arab integration into British society, I lost them there and then. Faiza had lived the previous seventeen years in Liverpool utterly dependent on her husband for all financial and practical concerns. I helped as much as I could when I lived in England. Now, with husband gone and brother away, came the time for Faiza to show some independence and decide what to do with the business. And because she really lived in England in name only, she had no choice but to sell everything and move back to Yemen. Running a business when you hadn't learned enough about it, or about the language in which it was conducted, was not an option. Not even offers from other Yemeni expatriates to help manage the store—which by that

stage included a liquor licence that she found objectionable for religious reasons—could take the burden of such a task off her. She
had to join her sisters in a culture that she understood best. What a
waste of a British passport, I often thought.

BY THE END OF 1999 I qualified for Canadian citizenship. I wanted
it so badly for one reason: Canada, or at least Toronto, was *home*.
It was the fifth country I had lived in but the one that welcomed
me the most. I loved its liberal society and what was then its neutral stance in the Middle East. I consider myself very lucky to have
landed in Canada during the tenure of a Liberal government. I
would have got a completely different impression of the country
and its culture had I arrived here on Stephen Harper's watch. I
certainly wouldn't have felt as welcome as an immigrant of Arab
origin. On a more practical note, travelling on a Yemeni passport,
especially to the US, took the fun out of any holiday plans. I'd go
early to the airport, but I'd still miss my flight to New York or Los
Angeles because I'd be pulled aside for questioning. I could see no
benefit in continuing to hold that passport if I didn't have to. Technically, it was the only official connection between my homeland
and me, and I'd checked out of that country many years ago. In
fact, I checked out of the Arab world as soon as I first arrived
in England in the late 1980s. I couldn't wait to get my Canadian
citizenship, and in the summer of 2000 I did, at a swearing-in ceremony at St. Clair Avenue and Yonge Street in midtown Toronto. I
was in the middle of covering the Toronto Fringe Festival for *Eye
Weekly* but wouldn't have missed that ceremony for the world. I
invited my dear friend Shane, himself an immigrant from Australia and now a naturalized Canadian. We were the poster boys for
immigration, we joked.

Home at last. I was Canadian now and proud of it. I'd reached my final destination after three decades of travelling and relocating, with my family and alone. Not only that, but I was settling into a city that had given me so much in such a short time—a home, a social life, a partner and above all a place to be who I was, without fear, shame or risk of life.

The only snag was that I got laid off the same summer from the online agency and faced more months of unemployment. I hated that job, but at least it provided a regular paycheque. I was better prepared this time. I had some contacts for freelance writing; I had put away some money in a savings account; and I had a partner to look after me if I needed it. But I knew one thing about myself: I liked the security of a paycheque, no matter how small, and I wasn't one for hustling as a freelancer. When my editor at *Eye Weekly* mentioned that the *Globe and Mail*'s *Report on Business* magazine was looking for a production editor, I wasn't sure what that meant, but I made the call to the contact there. In twenty-four hours I had a job interview and an offer to start immediately. I think the editors there were desperate to find someone to take the job, and I was desperate for one. Perfect match. Desperation worked to my advantage again. Because of my copyediting experience, I picked up the intricacies of production editing very quickly. Working at the *Globe and Mail*— the paper I was told to check out at Canada House in London if I wanted to learn more about Canada—was the chance of a lifetime for someone whose career was now focused on journalism.

My charmed life in Toronto continued. The *Globe* job qualified as a crash course in professional journalism, and I shared it with a great team. The hours were long, but I lived just a few streetcar stops away, so no commuting to add to my day like some of my colleagues. I was freelancing more for *Eye Weekly* and establishing my name as a theatre critic. I liked the low-key and accessible nature of local Toronto theatre. Soon thereafter I started writing for *Globe Television,* the newspaper's TV magazine, and an editor at the soon-to-be-launched *Elle Canada* approached me to become their regular theatre contributor. That dream I had when I boarded the plane for Toronto had come true: I'd carved out an alternative family and tradition for myself. I never understood, and will never be able to, all the Toronto bashing from those who live outside it. I don't know if there's a special trick or magic formula to living here. The way the city opened its doors to me makes me think it's their loss.

It was perhaps too good to be true. And I may have jinxed it all by succumbing to family pressure to visit them in Yemen—for the first time in nearly eight years. Having been away for so long, there was no need for me to worry any longer about the unspoken issue of my sexuality. The less they knew about my life, the happier they and I were. My friends would often ask me to explain how I came out to my family, given their religious and social views. The truth is that I never did. The whole coming out scene—the "Mom, Dad, I have something to tell you" scenario—is part of the Western narrative of being gay. My sisters in particular figured it out soon enough without me having to come out. They dealt with it by either ignoring it or by telling extended family members to leave me alone whenever any of them suggested a suitable bride.

In the summer of 2001 I made the trip back home. I don't think any phone conversation or letter could have prepared me for what I experienced there.

CHAPTER ELEVEN

CANADA

Reality

No wonder there are very few direct flights from Toronto to virtually anywhere in the Arab world now, and none back in 2001. You need a connection in that middle ground of Europe to link the two. That's what I was thinking when I reached Sana'a, after a long stopover in Frankfurt. It's difficult to explain the feeling I, as an Arab person, get whenever I visit the Middle East, and especially Yemen. There's a sickness in the belly, a nervousness all over. Every trip back could turn into a long-term prison sentence. The prison could be emotional, as I confront a family that has changed and is visibly suffering, trapping me in guilt and uncertainty. Or physical, should the temperamental government declare me an abomination for writing in gay magazines or curating a program of short films for a gay and lesbian film festival. I realize it's my paranoia, and I've probably inherited it from my own father, but this is not what going home should feel like. And who's to say that this is home, except in a blood memory sort of way? My roots are in Yemen, but everything else remains firmly fixed in Canada, my real home.

At the immigration booth my worst fears were confirmed. I was flying on my Canadian passport, which clearly stated Aden as my place of birth. According to a staffer at the Yemeni embassy in Ottawa, I didn't need a visa if my passport spelled that out. The officer checking my passport at Sana'a International Airport hemmed and hawed about the fact that I should have applied for a visa. Although I didn't believe a word of it, I protested that this was my homeland and I had the right to visit my family whenever I wanted. The usual barrage of questions followed. Where did my family live? I honestly wasn't sure, as houses in Sana'a didn't always have street numbers. It was somewhere on the Ring Road in the Hasaba district, I replied. When did I last see them? About eight years before. Why so long?

That I couldn't answer in a sentence or two. Eventually, he let me in, but asked that I register with local security as an alien. Finally we were in agreement on something. At Customs, the security guard asked why I had brought so much chocolate with me all the way from Canada. It was the only request from my sisters for their children. Most of the chocolate sold in local stores tasted stale or was too expensive to be a daily treat.

Khairy waited for me at the arrivals gate. The drive home took longer than usual. Traffic had something to do with it. Even more cars, more people. We didn't pass an intersection without a filthy-looking child or an older bedraggled woman begging for money. "Displaced Iraqis," my brother explained, in case I thought they were native Yemenis. Then he broke it to me. "I want you to be prepared when we get home. Things have got a bit difficult for the family." That sickness in my stomach returned instantly. I asked him to elaborate. "You'll see." His tone was that of an older brother providing counsel, but it contained hints of a resentment that the passage of time had not eased. After all, I was the one who'd selfishly thought I deserved better than the rest of my family and had chosen a different life for myself. I'd also refused to visit them for so many years, despite several invitations. They took it personally, and I didn't blame them.

Posing with my closest sisters, Ferial (right) and Hoda, while holding my nephew Motaz in Sana'a in 2001. It was the last time I saw Ferial, who died a year later from a brain aneurism.

The changes Khairy had tried to prepare me for were easy to spot. It was more than simply the passage of time. Two of my sisters—Hoda and Ferial—were thin to the point of looking sick and anemic. Hoda was only forty-six but was missing half her teeth and using dentures. Ferial, fifty, had lost her job at the USAID after the USS *Cole* incident and suffered a deep and long depression, in a country that barely recognized mental health issues or knew how to deal with them. The idea of therapy would sit alongside Botox or liposuction as an example of Western vanity and decadence, even though our father relied on counselling in the 1970s to get over his losses. Raja'a, forty-two, had gone from wearing the hijab to a full-scale niqab, where only her eyes were visible. She said she preferred the anonymity it gave her. Still working as a librarian at Sana'a University, she occasionally got stopped by students in the market if she wasn't wearing the niqab, just for a chat or to ask library-related questions. She said the niqab made her feel more mobile, free to move from one store to the next. I didn't think that was a good excuse, but wearing it was not just camouflage to her. It felt right, she said.

As for my mother, I hid a sigh when I saw her hunched walk and wrinkled face. She could only get from her room to the bathroom or kitchen by holding on to the walls for support. My sisters would take turns ensuring that the bathroom floor was dry, as a slip could be fatal. She was just seventy. Years of inadequate medical care, intense political and social pressures after the civil war ended in 1994 and various family arguments after my father's death had taken a toll on everyone. But my mother seemed to have borne the brunt of it.

The men hadn't fared much better. As Helmi told me, raising a family in Sana'a was a daily challenge. Public schools are under-funded, there were no playgrounds for children to be children—and God forbid any one of them got seriously sick. You took your life in your hands every time you went to a hospital in Sana'a. "You've escaped all this," he said. I answered with a simple "Can you blame me?" While deep down I didn't think they really did, there seemed to be a collective will to punish me for abandoning them. At least Faiza had returned home when her life in England came to what the family might call a natural end. When I showed them copies of *Elle Canada* magazine and a few of my *Eye Weekly* and *Globe* stories, they seemed less impressed and more concerned with the fact that someone with a Ph.D. in English made a living out of writing for newspapers and magazines. It seemed so beneath my education, and in a field not worthy of a Muslim's attention. If they asked me any questions at all about my career choices, they tended to focus on how I made money or spent it.

It seemed we needed an interpreter—someone who could explain to them how my life had panned out in Canada and, in turn, tell me how theirs had unfolded against Yemen's many crises. I understood the words they were saying, but my mind couldn't piece together their meanings. It wasn't very long before I started counting the hours until bedtime so I could get relief from our struggle to comprehend one another.

But it was the level of religiosity that truly startled me. My sisters were checking in on each other to make sure they prayed. When the TV was not tuned to Egyptian or Lebanese soap operas, it was on networks as diverse as Al Jazeera and Al-Manar, the latter the PR wing of Hezbollah. It was on one of Al-Manar's programs that I encountered the name Osama bin Laden for the first time. I don't think I had heard of him before. He was presented not as a threat but as one of the forces that were keeping the West worried about the return to Islam. I made no note of it. Just another radical jihadist from Saudi Arabia's elite—a spoiled rich kid who needed a cause to latch on to.

In the past, we'd all watched Hollywood movies or TV shows as a family, but now, despite all the TV watching, there seemed to be very little room for curiosity about the Western world. We'd grown up on episodes of *The Rockford Files*, *Columbo* and *The Bionic Woman* on the American side, and *Upstairs Downstairs* on the British. Classic Hollywood movies from the 1940s and '50s were essential viewing. *Now, Voyager*, starring Bette Davis, had become a firm favourite for me and my sisters. Ferial loved Humphrey Bogart; I, Claudette Colbert.

I did notice that my nieces had a passing interest in episodes of *Friends,* which some Gulf TV station showed with Arabic subtitles. I don't know if they ever saw the episode where Chandler pretends to be going to Yemen to escape the annoying and persistent girl-friend Janice. Joey, the Italian jock in the show, congratulates Chandler on choosing a name that sounds like a real country.

Attempts to engage my sisters in old stories about life in Cairo or Beirut were successful, but would be followed with remarks like, "Those days are long gone." We'd talk, at first tentatively, and then they'd open up until they got too nostalgic and teary eyed. This happened whenever we went through old family photos, of which there must have been hundreds. My father had insisted on a pic-torial record of his children's lives—a tradition that stopped a few years after the family moved to Sana'a. It was as if the new life was not worth documenting. I saw the look on my sisters' faces as they gazed at their younger selves. Pictures of them in swimsuits on our summer vacations in Alexandria were quickly thrown back to the bottom of the pile. It was one thing to see their younger selves but another to recall the freedoms that came with that youth. Later dur-ing that visit, I put a handful of those old black-and-white photos in an envelope and dropped it in my briefcase. I had an unsettling fear that my sisters themselves or one of my brothers would destroy the photos. (So far this hasn't happened, but I know that when I published one of them many years later for a *Globe and Mail* article, they were mad at me for months.)

I tried to find something that connected the pictures with the flesh and blood. And yes, there were traces of my old girls. The same generosity with whatever little cash they had. Hoda spent most of her salary buying clothes and toys for her nephews and nieces, whose parents were struggling just to house and feed them. Every few months, rent from properties in Aden that my uncle there collected and sent in moneybags with trusted travellers on a bus (can you imagine that?) was distributed evenly among the siblings, but in months when one of my brothers was going through a rough patch—a sick child, unemployment, overdue tuition—my sisters were the first to pass along their share to whoever needed it the most. Despite such generosity, money turned into a constant source of argument and stress. Over here, we'd turn to credit cards, overdrafts and lines of credit to make up the shortfall. None of my siblings had a credit card or an overdraft. Receiving a line of credit was simply accepting money from one brother or sister and repaying it if and when the situation changed. Even my mother, who seemed to have forgotten much of her past life, got involved in discussions about money and expenses. She felt that the little that my sisters bought for themselves was excessive and a sign of vanity. They started hiding from Safia whatever they bought, or only indulging in small things she wouldn't notice: earrings or perfume.

Like my sisters, Safia rarely discussed the past and lived for the present. My father's name was mentioned only once and in passing; she still blamed him for dragging the family back to Yemen. The past came with too heavy an emotional cost to relive. And the future as a concept was loaded with worry about a country that had been spiralling deeper into debt and poverty for over a decade. Safia seemed content to live in her room and watch TV for hours. Her last outing had been a trip to the dentist nearly six months before. I still remember how nice she always smelled during my visit, even though she couldn't take a daily bath anymore. Still, she insisted on changing her clothes and using traditional scents to keep herself refreshed. She looked somewhat self-conscious about using her hands to eat in front of me instead of the spoon that my father taught her to use when she was a young mother. She refused to let me drink tap water in case I got sick, but she herself wouldn't touch the bottled water. A waste of money, she'd say. A week into my visit she noticed that Motaz, my partner in Canada, was calling every few days. "He must really love you," she said in as neutral a statement as she could muster. I don't know if by then she'd really figured out my true relationship, but that remains my only delightful memory of that difficult trip.

The most difficult part, however, came halfway through it when Helmi insisted that I visit my father's grave and say the traditional prayer for the dead—the *fatiha,* the opening chapter of the Quran, which by that point I had forgotten and had no desire to recite. I protested as much as I could, but he wouldn't listen to any objection. To him, going back to Canada without making that pilgrimage was one act of defiance he wouldn't tolerate. The entire visit took less than five minutes. It was an unmarked grave near the very front of an unremarkable burial ground. The local guard guided us to it, while children and poor widows stood nearby waiting for us to hand over alms. Once again, I felt like a voyeur on a scene of my own life. Wasn't I just buying a round of drinks at a bar on Queen Street in Toronto only two weeks before? Wasn't my biggest decision back then whether to take a cab home or wait for the streetcar? How had I suddenly found myself standing in a cemetery on the edge of Sana'a with a brother who proceeded to recite from the Quran as the un-merry widows waited for handouts? Something told me that even my father—the old Mohamed, who was chased out of Aden apartments by angry fathers and husbands and who took pride in speaking like an Englishman—would have found that scene a little too operatic. He would probably have told me to go home and salvage the rest of the day. I'd agree, but to me going home meant boarding a plane back to Frankfurt and connecting with the first flight home to Toronto, where I got to review performances and not act in them.

I returned to Toronto late in July with a heavy heart and an unspeakable sadness, but also with one more affirmation that my world and my family's had diverged so totally that there could never be a chance of reconnecting. There was no more halfway point like my sister's place in Liverpool. The pressures of that visit showed up in my relationship with Motaz, which went into two years of on-again, off-again, until it was over for good. He remained part of my Toronto family for a few more years until he decided to go to Beirut and give up his dreams of making it as a choreographer. Emotionally, I was too exhausted to consider giving or receiving love. It was easier to think of the difference between me and the family in intellectual terms and from a certain safe distance. To return from Yemen and in forty-eight hours be sitting in a Toronto theatre reviewing a classic production at Harbourfront or interviewing celebrities for *Globe Television* magazine sometimes was more than my mind could comprehend. The two lives couldn't coexist. One of them had to be killed off, for good this time.

I resolved to snap out of this Yemen-induced funk by refocusing on my life as a Canadian. Not an Arab-Canadian but just a Canadian. I would read more Canadian history and literature. I'd even watch made-in-Canada movies and TV dramas—most of which I found utterly cold and soulless, but at least they were Canadian.

It was a short-lived resolution. Just six weeks later, September 11 changed everything.

I WAS WORKING OUT at a gym near the *Globe and Mail* offices on Front and Spadina when the first plane hit the World Trade Center that Tuesday morning. My trainer, Mike, thought it was just a little private jet that had flown lower than it should. When the second plane crashed into the other tower and the news anchor—it was CNN, I believe—declared it was no accident but a deliberate terrorist attack, I blurted, "Oh, God, please don't let it be Muslims or Arabs." I knew immediately that an event like this would change everything for all parties, including, of course, North Americans of Arab origin like me. Bizarrely enough, I continued with the workout until 10 a.m. Mike wouldn't let me use a terrorist attack as an excuse to mess up our appointment schedule. By the time I got to work half an hour later, the second tower had already collapsed.

So much has been written from the perspective of Americans who either had friends or families in the towers (and elsewhere) that day, or who were among the millions who simply watched the attack unfold on TV. But to be an Arab in North America at the time meant that the horror of those events was coupled with fear of repercussions, retaliations, discrimination or a combination of all three—just because we shared the same heritage as the hijackers. If my heart beat a little faster every time I crossed borders before 9/11, it now raced with fear. Once again, Toronto came through for me. All my fears about being verbally or physically assaulted—very real possibilities had I been living in parts of the UK or the US, and possibly other parts of Canada—came to nothing. Apart from the odd stare every now and then on the subway or on an elevator in a high-rise, my day-to-day life was not affected.

But on a more profound level I *was* affected, in ways that only a few weeks before I would have found unimaginable. I'd spent almost two decades trying to distance myself from my Arab and Muslim identities and cultivating a Western one. Now the world seemed divided along those very lines. I felt compelled to show somehow that there was more to where I came from than terrorism and strict readings of Islam. I didn't really want to be an ambassador for Arab culture, but no longer could I sit out that debate.

At the *Globe and Mail,* I was sent to report on what was going on in mosques around the Greater Toronto Area, since I could blend in with the crowd of worshippers. I hadn't stepped inside a mosque since I was probably sixteen or seventeen, and here I was, twenty years later, spying on Canadian Muslims. On the eve of the invasion of Iraq in 2003, the paper sent me to Chicago and Detroit to cover the responses of the largest Arab communities in North America. I loitered outside a mosque in suburban Chicago before I stepped in. I think the imam there was more concerned about the parking situation than terrorism. Many in the Arab American community there shared with me their fears of reprisals or attacks against their businesses or families, which made me even more grateful to be living in Toronto. I then went to Detroit to write about the life of a Yemeni American soldier who was training to join the US-led coalition forces in Iraq. In Dearborn, Michigan, I found myself sitting in a Yemeni restaurant ordering the same old food that my family was probably serving for lunch. So much for killing off that part of my life.

The first anniversary of 9/11, however, came with devastating news. I woke up at 6 a.m. to the phone ringing. I assumed it was a wrong number, ignored it and went back to sleep. I'd trained my family to bear in mind the time difference and not call that early. When the phone rang again a few minutes later, I picked it up and immediately recognized Wahbi's voice on the other end. "Kamal, be strong. I have bad news." I assumed it was my mother. To my shock, he told me it was Ferial. She had died from a brain aneurism two days earlier. They'd waited until after the funeral to let me know.

I knew how unhappy she had been since losing her USAID job. She had struggled for years between unemployment and another job that she accepted out of desperation. She hated not having her own income and, like our father, was running through her rainy-day savings much faster than she thought she would be because of the inflation in Yemen. When I had last seen her, the year before, I could immediately sense her profound sadness. But I shied away from asking her to confide in me or urging her to consider anti-depressants. I just didn't have the courage or the will to enter into any such discussion.

Ferial's mental problems coincided with some physical ones. She'd inherited the same arthritic condition that my mother suffered from, and only a few months before had travelled to Cairo for a pair of routine medical procedures. That's what people in Yemen who can afford it do—seek medical advice in the nearest, relatively more developed, Arab country. As far as we knew, both procedures went well, and the fact that she could walk more comfortably made her happier. Ferial had felt more positive about herself, said my sister Farida, who accompanied her to various medical appointments in Cairo. No one knew what one factor, if any, triggered the aneurism that caused her death. It didn't matter. Six years after my father's death, Yemen had claimed one of my sisters. My resentment towards that country for what it had done to the family intensified from that moment on.

I HAD NO INTENTION of going back to Yemen after that stressful 2001 visit. The flights from Toronto were physically exhausting, and once I reached my destination I knew there would be emotional strain. But it didn't sound like my mother's body could handle its various pains and aches, and her mind was deeply affected by the death of her favourite daughter. She never fully recovered from that loss. For almost seven years she'd dream about her "white child" (Ferial was very light skinned) and wake up crying. At the insistence of my brothers and sisters, I made another trip to the Middle East in 2006. This time, in an attempt to create an emotional buffer, I bookended the visit to Sana'a with a short visit to Beirut and an overnight in Cairo. In effect, I embarked on a trip along the course of my early life. But the main purpose was to see my mother. Even though I talked to her on the phone almost every other week, I knew she was not quite there by then, as she'd occasionally end our talks with "Say hello to the kids." Previous trips to the Middle East had left me shattered, but I rebounded. Not this time. That trip in 2006 triggered a depression that took me almost four years and a lot of willpower to recover from. I experienced in person what I only knew in theory five years earlier when I detected it in my sister.

If things were not considerably worse than they had been five years before, it was because suffering has a tendency to plateau. Even in Yemen. My family had found ways to adapt to Yemen in the past, but they were mainly psychological ways. Now life required some practical skills that they had to acquire. Water was now in such short supply that its main source became private sellers who roamed up and down the streets and filled up residents' private tanks at a premium. Hoda became a pro at flagging them down in the main street and guiding them to our home. She'd then connect the water line to their tank. I had no idea how she knew how much water was enough, but she figured it out. Similarly, Khairy had given up on the government supplying his electricity and invested in a generator. So much food was spoiled and so many football games were missed as he—and everybody else—sat in the dark during the now-regular power outages.

My sister Raja'a played a trick on me one weekday afternoon. She spotted me walking back from the university where she worked and, to see how long it would be before I recognizd her, decided to follow me without revealing herself. She waited outside when I went into a store and continued to walk behind me once I came out. She was wearing a niqab that covered everything but her eyes. Only when I made a turn that led to our street did I cotton on. It was meant as a joke, but as I later tried to explain the encounter to my Toronto friends, I (and they) didn't see a funny side to it. Neither did I see a logical reason for my brothers' objection to a few family pictures of my sisters with their hair showing. "What if the man developing the film at the camera shop saw your sisters' uncovered heads?" they asked me. The pictures from that trip are locked in a filing cabinet in my Toronto apartment. Not even my dearest friends have seen them and I rarely look at them. They represent a descent into a world that, to me, is intolerable.

I took this photo of my nieces Nagala (left) and Yousra during a day trip just outside Sana'a in 2006. My nephews Motaz and Mohamed stand in the middle. Even as teenagers, the women were expected to cover up. It was a far cry from what their aunts and mothers had worn at the same age.

During that visit, I detected the impact of Yemen on my nephews and nieces, who were too young in 2001 for me to register their attitude to life. My niece Nagala, who was now nineteen, reminded me of my younger self. She loved American TV and spoke fluent, accent-free English. She asked me if I had friends and if so what was that like? She didn't have any, as she spent most of her evenings looking after her younger brother while her mother, Hanna, worked at a night school. She realized that going to university would be difficult with this schedule but was determined to study for a degree in English. I hope it provides her with the escape route it's given me, but the odds are against her. Her father was usually chewing khat or asleep all day. His life had not changed in any way in the last two decades. Another niece, Yousra, was trying to rebel against her mother's autocratic and Islamic upbringing, but that was causing serious confrontations between them. Every time I weighed in, I got a strong "None of your business" from her mother, Raja'a. I couldn't counter that. I have made it my business not to get involved or be a part of their lives. Like many teenagers, Yousra loved going to the mall and eating fast food. My fondest memory of that visit was going for frozen fruit drinks with her mother. The sight of Raja'a lifting up the niqab to sip on her cup was part comedy, part a socio-economic snapshot of life in Yemen. As for my nephew Motaz, his father has ignored him because he likes crazy things like the internet, loud music and colourful shirts. He was my main guide to the new Sana'a, where malls and mullahs shared the same space. The president's way of pacifying his public was to distract them with more commercial enterprises. More malls than hospitals had been built in the previous ten years, I was informed.

I told each one of my nephews and nieces individually that if they wanted to follow my example, they'd have to finish their education and get out of Yemen as fast as they could. But their emotional bonds with their parents and their brothers and sisters were much stronger than mine ever had been twenty-five years ago. They wanted change, but they were not willing to abandon everything they knew and loved (and even hated) for it. I didn't know it then, but what I was witnessing in Nagala, Yousra and Motaz were the seeds of the revolution that swept through Yemen and elsewhere in the Arab world in 2011.

CHAPTER TWELVE

ARAB WORLD

Revolution

In the last months leading up to her death in October 2009, Safia struggled to complete a single phone conversation. When I called, one of my sisters would put the phone to her ear so she could at least hear my voice. I'd say a few hellos and how are yous? She said nothing in return. I spent much of 2008 and 2009 expecting that early-morning call to tell me that she had passed away. To me, she was already dead and lived in my memories and photographs only. When that call actually came, I was prepared emotionally for the news and for the realization that with Safia gone I had lost the strongest and final bond with my siblings.

I felt sad but relieved.

By then it had become clear to them and to me that our relationship was broken beyond repair. Without my mother's health to discuss, the phone calls lasted for a few awkward moments before time ran out on their phone card—they didn't have international dialling from the home phone—or I made an excuse to end the call. Because they made most of their calls on a Sunday, I began to dread the weekend. When I remembered, I would turn off the ringer before I went to bed on Saturday. I'd go months without making calls myself. I found that dialling the country code for Yemen was the first step towards a world I wanted more than anything to pretend did not exist. I just wanted to resume the life I had before the last two visits and before 9/11. And for the most part, I did. I sold my downtown condo shortly after Safia's death and moved to a different one, just to make my plans for new beginnings more formal and concrete. My initial concept for this book was as an elegy not for my dead parents but my living siblings. I mourned their lost lives but wanted to keep mine moving forward.

All my plans were shattered in early January 2010 and, after a short lull, the first few months of 2011. After years of Yemen being an "in other news" segment on newscasts, the country captured world attention in December 2009 when a Nigerian-born member of al Qaeda in the Arabian Peninsula tried to blow up a US-bound jet with explosives hidden in his briefs. News reports revealed that the underwear bomber, as he came to be known, was trained in Yemen. All of a sudden, Yemen emerged as a new frontline of terror—a failed state where the rule of President Saleh hardly extended outside the major four cities of Sana'a, Taiz and Hodeidah in the north and, to a lesser extent, Aden in the south. As a Yemeni person living abroad and despite the bad publicity, I welcomed the focus on Yemen, a country that very few people understood and fewer still had ventured into. For the first time in my life I wrote, in broad strokes in the *Globe and Mail*, about the changed lives of my siblings. Even my closest friends knew very little of this side of my life, which I kept either in low profile or a complete secret. I had hoped that the new spotlight would convince both the World Bank and other Arab countries to lend a hand to a place that, famously, was projected to be the first in the world to run out of water and had been officially designated as one of the poorest in the Arab world. World attention on Yemen was intense but sadly brief. By the middle of January, the devastating earthquake in Haiti shifted global attention to that tragedy and Yemen slipped out of the headlines. Only those with strong interest in security and terrorism issues managed to keep up with the realities of life in Yemen. Some frightening details emerged.

Al Qaeda and its affiliates had established a small but powerful base in the country, which Saleh then used as an excuse to shake down the US government for some war-on-terror cash. In the south, the old socialist holdouts that Saleh had oppressed for two decades regrouped and launched a secessionist campaign against the government. Elsewhere tribal conflicts and land disputes meant that more resources were being directed towards quelling or containing armed conflicts than towards health, education or social-assistance programs. I could tell that poverty had spread further just by reading or watching the news reports. Sana'a looked even more dilapidated than it had a few years before. The clock seemed to be going backward in that part of the Arab world.

Despite the raging pocket wars and crumbling infrastructure, for most Yemenis, including my family, life continued as normal. They'd learned to cope with the usual shortages of water and electricity, and the staggering unemployment rate hovered around 20 to 25 percent. My sister Hoda had been working on a contract basis for almost ten years but was forced to quit her job to become Safia's primary caregiver in late 2008. When she tried to return to work after Safia's death, she came face to face with the realities of the new job market. Her thirty years of work experience didn't give her any edge over the flood of applicants for every job. Yemen had expanded its post-secondary education in the last ten years, opening its doors to private and foreign institutions after decades of just a handful of government-run universities in the major cities. It was an attempt to absorb the population explosion of the 1990s and to make university education available to as large a segment of society as possible. The initiative was well-intentioned, but with a stalling and corrupt economy, most of these graduates ended up either unemployed or completely underemployed. Those who were still in university, like my own nephews and nieces, knew that there was nothing awaiting them after graduation, so they kept enrolling in more classes.

Egypt has gone through the same population shift and expansion in higher education. The same younger generation by and large orchestrated the protests in Tahrir Square in Cairo and inspired similar demonstrations in Sana'a and Taiz.

I must admit I was hoping that the wave of uprisings wouldn't reach Yemen, to a large extent because I didn't want to think about what weeks—and I thought it would be a matter of weeks—of civil unrest would do to the already low standard of living and the fragile economy. I'd be lying if I said I wasn't trying to avoid having to think of the gap between my world and that of my siblings. I didn't want to revisit the guilt, discomfort and sadness I experienced whenever my family came into my Canadian life. The quieter things seemed, the more distant the problems became. I envied my Canadian friends whose family stories involved normal events like visiting the parents at the cottage, attending cousins' weddings or planning a Thanksgiving meal. My family life always seemed complicated and on the edge of chaos. Indeed, the protests in Sana'a reached a boiling point in late spring of 2011 before the country descended into a full-fledged civil war between Saleh's loyalists and the main army of the opposition movement in June.

By then my concerns for the family outweighed my selfishness (and there's no other word for it; I toyed with saying self-protection) and their safety became my number-one concern. Our new family home happened to be just a mile or two away from our old Hasaba district, where the most intense fighting took place. During the worst phase of the war, my sisters Faiza and Hoda sought shelter in my niece's house in a relatively remote part of town. Raja'a and Hanna and their children hid in my brother Khairy's place in the suburbs. Wahbi was too proud to impose his three young boys on anyone and held out at the family home, where he lived on the third floor, for as long as he could. I just couldn't make sense of the contrast. Here I was, walking my dog in peaceful midtown Toronto on beautiful spring days, when my own brother had no option but to stay put at home even as gunfights could be heard and the occasional rocket launched a few blocks away. The fact that they had experienced it all before in 1994 made little difference. The new war lasted for about three weeks, during which the nature of our phone conversations—and my entire relationship with the family—changed.

I had always been able to hear them but not really feel what they went through. Until now. They felt abandoned, betrayed, both by Yemen and the Arab world. Hanna, with whom I rarely ever talked, wept uncontrollably when recounting how her son, age twelve, lost the ability to sleep after several nights of bombings and gunshots. "No one will save us," she lamented. Faiza told me how they had to make the most of their three to four hours of electricity every day. No matter what time it was, when the electricity came on they would cook lunch or dinner, since there was no natural light in the kitchen. They avoided buying any food that would spoil too quickly, like fish. Sometimes, when they didn't time it properly, they'd have to grind spices or prepare other ingredients by hand, taking them hours instead of minutes in the blender. "We've gone back to the time of our grandparents," Faiza complained. Whenever I suggested they sit out the war in Cairo, both Raja'a and Hoda responded as if I'd asked them to relocate to the moon. "Where would we stay? Who's going to pay for it?" I offered to help, but they declined. Part of this was a martyrdom I'd got used to, and part just anger and stubbornness, which was new to me.

One of their top concerns was leaving the family home unattended. When the fighting got even closer to our part of Sana'a, Wahbi relented and booked his family into a hotel room for a few nights. First, he had to find a trusted night guard to keep an eye on the house. It wasn't that uncommon for military or tribal chiefs in Sana'a to simply occupy an empty house and take ownership of it. I remembered my father's mantra about the lack of stability in the Middle East, which was the main reason he never bought any properties after his were seized in 1967. He knew that to live in the Middle East was to accept a life on the run. It was easier to run when you rented someone else's house, he said. In fact, we'd only bought this house for the family in 2004, long after he and my sister Ferial died.

When a ceasefire of sorts came into effect in late June, my siblings returned to the family home, but day-to-day living became even more intolerable. Protests and isolated armed clashes would erupt at any minute. A simple shopping trip became an elaborate operation that involved plotting escape routes and bringing extra money in case they had to abandon the car and find a cab driver willing to take them as close as possible to home. Food prices had shot up, and drivers lined up, sometimes for a full day, just to fill up gas tanks. After a few days of normal service, electricity was again reduced to the now-normal handful of hours. With the exception of Raja'a, who worked at the university—the Tahrir Square of Sana'a— they all returned to work. "Good days and bad days" was how Hoda described the situation to me on the phone. What happened in any given day depended on the night before. A quiet night with no machine guns meant a peaceful morning when they could go to work or get groceries. Hoda was lucky in that the one job she was able to find the previous year was within a short walking distance from home. Even after they bought a generator, finding enough gas to run it was difficult. When they did, it extended their access to electricity by a handful of hours every day.

My niece Yousra, by then twenty-three, would go behind her mother's back to the protests outside Sana'a University and demand political and economic change. In an email message to me she explained why she insisted on speaking her mind in this way: "I'm a Yemeni and I have a right." I couldn't imagine taking part in a revolution or even a demand for change when I was her age. All I'd wanted was to get out. That email highlighted the differences between her generation and her mother's and mine. It's not just that technology has connected the youth of a country like Yemen, there comes a point when a population has just had enough of oppression and despair and decides to say or do something about it.

The rest of the summer passed relatively quietly. I planned a trip to check in on the family and to see first-hand the effects of the revolution on daily life in Yemen. I was going to visit during the month of Ramadan, which coincided with August 2011. They seemed optimistic enough that the worst was over and in early phone conversations were surprised but welcoming. As the visit got closer, their tone changed. Usually, they are the ones who insist I visit, but they seemed hesitant and nervous about it. "Put it off until later in the year," Wahbi suggested, adding that next summer would be even better. I told him that I had enough experience of travelling the world and could look after myself. "But you haven't been to Yemen lately," he said. When he handed me over to Faiza, she asked that I call Helmi before I get on a plane.

My conversations with Helmi had been strained for many years, but when we eventually talked later the same week, the full picture of what had been happening in Sana'a became clear. It wasn't just my safety that the family was worried about but the thought of me seeing them living in such primitive conditions. They couldn't shower as often as they used to and couldn't always spare enough water to wash vegetables as thoroughly. My brother was worried I might get sick. "You're not used to this, Kamal," he said. It took me back to my last visit, when my mother insisted that I drink bottled water and ordered my sisters to wash the food with it to make sure I didn't get any stomach bugs. Ever since that conversation with Helmi I haven't been able to turn on the tap or the lights in my Toronto home without realizing that these simple everyday acts are luxuries to my own family. I wish I had a more satisfactory explanation, but much of the distance I put between us and the alienation I cultivated towards them suddenly disappeared. Like a man obsessed, I looked online for news about Yemen every few hours. I considered it a good day when there was none. Whenever I saw the word "Yemen" on the home page of a website, my heart would sink. There hadn't been, and there may not be, any good news coming out of Yemen for a while.

In September, shortly after Ramadan, intense fighting between the revolutionaries and the Saleh loyalists resumed in Sana'a. Once again the family had to flee our home and seek temporary shelter with my brother. Even Wahbi swallowed his pride and took his kids to his brother-in-law's house. The schools, government buildings and business offices were closed, with only the food markets and some adventurous retailers staying open. Because I couldn't get through to any of them from Canada, I used my sister Farida in Cairo as a go-between, especially when I read about the sudden return of President Saleh to Sana'a after four months in Saudi Arabia. His comeback could either bring the civil war to a halt, at least a truce, or keep it raging indefinitely.

My Lebanese friends who have escaped the civil war in that country but left family members behind tell me that I'll get used to this feeling of helplessness and guilt. I don't know what to make of it. Does anyone ever accept that his family is suffering and living in the middle of a war zone? It was one thing to accept their conservatism and economically deprived condition. But a war? And even if the political and economic situation stabilizes, I have a feeling it will be too late for my brothers and sisters. Their generation has missed out. They enjoyed the first few years of the liberal and tolerant society of Aden, Beirut and Cairo, but the latter chapters of their lives have coincided with decades of political repression and religious dogma. I believe that my siblings have written off this life, hoping that they'll be rewarded in the afterlife, since they've been good and devout Muslims.

Just a few years ago I would have found that way of thinking not just defeatist but repellent. I can see it now as the natural conclusion of the intolerable journey they have been on. What started as the sectarian violence in Lebanon and continued with the rise of the Muslim Brotherhood in Egypt culminated with a civil war that grew out of Yemen's politically and religiously brutal society. I escaped, at least physically, but they had been paying for this trajectory for many years now. There might be hope for the new generation in Yemen and elsewhere in the Arab world, the generation of my younger nephews and nieces, but I think a lot more has to happen before there's any real change. It will take decades to reboot the economies of countries as different as Egypt and Yemen. It looks unlikely that foreign investment will flow back easily to Egypt, and it may not flow at all to Yemen, which had very little of it to begin with. Millions of unemployed and struggling youth could turn to hardline readings of Islam, leaving them vulnerable to extremists. I worry about the lives of women in a place like Yemen if that happens. How much more marginalized will they be? Despite the odd story in the Western media about how a handful of Yemeni women have taken part in, even spearheaded, the revolution, if the chaos continues the society that will emerge will be tribal, violent and hostile to women.

It has dawned on me that, despite the passage of time and the different specifics, what my family has been experiencing lately is but a replay of the troubles that started with our expulsion from Aden in 1967. History is repeating itself, but this time without my father to take the family out of harm's way and find temporary shelter. With my more comfortable income in Canada, I am in fact the best situated of all my siblings to play my father's role and airlift them to Cairo, which, despite its own post-revolution growing pains, remains the only relatively safe option. I can't believe that I'm even considering that possibility. Another relocation? And to Cairo?

Even Farida, who lives there, thinks that an exodus to Cairo is not a realistic option, given that there's no chance any of our siblings or their children will find work. The ongoing clashes between the army and the protestors, and the new outbreaks of sectarian violence between Muslims and Christians, mean that certain parts of Cairo are as dangerous as Sana'a.

Still, I feel they'd be safer in Cairo, assuming they'd be willing to budge on their resolution not to move. With twelve nephews and nieces and four spouses in addition to my eight siblings, moving the family would be much more difficult than it ever was for my father. And to move some of them and leave others to face their uncertain future would be unacceptable. "Either we all leave together or we stay together," Raja'a told me on the phone.

I became even more worried about them when news of the capture and death of Libya's Moammar Gadhafi broke in October 2011. Saleh and Gadhafi had a strong bond, and Gadhafi's death could strengthen both Saleh's resolve to stay in power by any means possible and the protestors' determination to oust him. To my family, the final outcome of the revolution isn't their main concern. All they want is to be able to live in their own home without waking up to gunshots or explosions. A home where running water and electricity are the norm and not the exception. It's great that a Yemeni revolutionary, Tawakel Karman, won the Nobel Peace Prize and that a handful of women burnt the veil—while fully veiled—in an act of defiance. All that plays well in Western media and helps advance the narrative of the Arab Spring. But none of it is keeping Yemeni families safe in their beds at night.

As a testament to their endurance and to prove that life must go on, even in the middle of a civil war, my family called with some good news: in late October, my nieces Yousra and Nagala had accepted marriage proposals from two eligible bachelors. In early December, the family enjoyed not one but two engagement parties. I'm relieved that the family can focus for now on new beginnings and happy occasions. In a recent phone call, my sister Hoda said that she's learned to sleep through late-night explosions. In the past, she'd get up and stay awake. Now she just goes back to bed as if she was woken up by a slamming door or the garbage truck.

After decades of periodically trying (and failing) to banish them from my thoughts, I think of my family all the time now. But I also think of how lucky and privileged I have been to come to Canada and make a home for myself here. The worse the situation gets in Yemen, the tighter I cling to my life in Toronto. The paranoid side of me still thinks that somehow even my Toronto existence may one day be taken away from me. The Middle East has a way of catching up with you no matter how far you run. I find it surreal that I'm writing about it now when in the past I didn't even want to speak the language or work on an Arab-themed art exhibit. And after decades of turning my back on Arab culture, I have rediscovered its music as if I'd never listened to it before. I love walking around

Toronto streets with old Egyptian music playing on my iPod. It has to be music from the 1950s to the early 1970s, a period that conjures up the glory days, when the family felt optimistic and protected even as the world around us was rapidly changing. I can't listen to any Egyptian music from the last twenty to twenty-five years, as it makes me think of nothing but cultural and emotional decline.

To me, the music I tried to escape is now a form of escapism. The '60s music of Abdel Halim Hafez, Shadia and Nagat play so well against the backdrop of the vast and safe streets of midtown Toronto, especially as I take my dog, Chester, for his long evening walks in the summer. "Why do you keep listening to that funny music?" a dog owner I often ran into in the park once asked me, as Shadia's voice filtered out of my headphones and into the warm summer air.

Long story.

ACKNOWLEDGEMENTS

Intolerable is about, for and because of my family. My late parents and sister Ferial will never get to read it, but I know that they've shaped my life and this narrative distillation of it. My remaining nine siblings and fourteen nephews and nieces have suffered silently for so long, but civil wars, crushing living conditions and political suppression have failed to change their close bond or love for one another—or for me, the proverbial black sheep, the one who left them behind. To them all, *salamati* and *hobbi*. I think of them every day.

My gratitude and admiration go to my gently tough editor, Jim Gifford, at HarperCollins Canada. In 2010 he was the first to react positively to my book proposal and he maintained that upbeat spirit for two full years. Jim was patient and understanding when I fell behind schedule and thorough and exacting (in a good, even great, way) whenever I handed over sample chapters or successive drafts. I couldn't have dreamed of a better editor for my first book. I asked him for some (platonic) handholding during our first in-person meeting, and he delivered. I'm also grateful to the incredibly meticulous Alex Schultz for copyediting—more like rescuing—the manuscript with such intelligence and sensitivity. He even corrected my spelling of Arabic words, a language he doesn't speak. Awesome. Thanks also to Lisa Rundle for her faith in my story and Noelle Zitzer for making the production stages of this book so easy on a nervous, habitually late and occasionally too-sick-to-work writer.

My agent, John Pearce, is another patient soul I've kept waiting while working and reworking my initial ideas for this book for over two years. He believed in what I wanted to write even when I had my own doubts. He urged me to open up and share my stories, and I'm so glad I took his advice. Our long lunches in Toronto's Boulevard Café on Harbord Street made me feel like a writer for the first time in my life. (Full disclosure: Moderate amounts of alcohol were consumed, possibly explaining that writerly feeling.)

The first person I ever discussed this book with was playwright and director Lee MacDougall during a summer afternoon chat in Stratford, Ontario. Thanks, Lee, for listening, encouraging and for suggesting Michael Ondaatje's *Running in the Family*. Pam Shime read an early draft of the proposal and tore most of my content to shreds. I couldn't be more grateful. My dear friend and role model Laurie Lynd, a gifted film and TV director, also read the proposal and added his visual panache and strong sense of story structure to it. His advice stuck in my head during the writing process. His later comments about the manuscript were equally insightful. I gave the manuscript to my brilliant friend Noreen Flanagan to read. She encouraged me to open up more emotionally, and I'm so glad I did. Her comments made me see parts of the story I, as a man, couldn't before.

The *Globe and Mail*'s Focus section, and particularly its editor in 2010, Carol Toller, commissioned the first outing of *Intolerable* as a two-thousand-word article, "From Bikinis to Burkas." I'm indebted to Carol not just for picking up my pitch but for giving the final piece its shape and emotional texture. The forty-eight hours we worked together were the most intense and rewarding in my life as a journalist. In a career with over fifteen hundred bylines, the final story was by far my most read and discussed. As it went viral, I felt part of a worldwide conversation about Islam, the Middle East and social change. Thanks to everyone who emailed me, sent a message on Facebook or added a comment on the *Globe*'s website. Thanks to Stephen Northfield, Jill Borra and Gabe Gonda, also from the *Globe and Mail*, for commissioning a piece about Cairo in early 2011, and to Rachel Giese and Alexandra Molotkow from the *Walrus* magazine for the opportunity to write about Yemen in the spring of the same year. Excerpts from all three pieces appear at different points in this book.

My colleagues at Ryerson University's School of Journalism deserve special thanks for supporting this book, which I first mentioned as a dream project in my job interview in May 2007. While much of that support was emotional and intellectual, I was also fortunate enough to receive financial aid from the Faculty of Communication and Design's Creative Grant program, which covered part of the cost of a trip back to Cairo and Beirut in 2010. Thanks to Dean Gerd Hauck and associate deans Abby Goodrum and Gillian Mothersill for the financial assistance.

My many students, especially in the master's of journalism class in magazine and feature writing in winter 2011, have heard me talk about the struggle to write a book while holding a teaching job. Thank you all for listening and for being such wonderful, resourceful and talented journalists.

As the book's dedication to Toronto suggests, I'm in love with this city (and this great country), but it shares my affection with another place thousands of miles away: Hong Kong. I don't think I could have finished this book without a two-week working holiday (and fourth visit in seven years) to Hong Kong in the spring of 2011. Maybe it's the former-colony thing, or perhaps it's just the city's seductive buzz and optimism that proved so inspiring. Either way, I'm thankful and lucky to have such a gorgeous home away from home.

Finally, I'm extremely fortunate in having so many lovely and kind friends in my life in Toronto and elsewhere. I made a decision not to list any by name for fear of forgetting someone, but they all know who they are. Thank you for being not just my friends but my second—and, at many times in my life, only—family. Almost all of you are reading about my pre-West life for the first time, which is an indication of how difficult it's been for me to discuss the past—and to write about it here. I hope *Intolerable* will explain why I've often stayed silent or avoided the subject of my (and my blood family's) history.

Love, peace and freedom of choice to one and all.

—Toronto, January 2012

ABOUT THE AUTHOR

Kamal Al-Solaylee, an associate professor and undergraduate program director at the School of Journalism at Ryerson University, was previously a theatre critic at Canada's national newspaper the *Globe and Mail*. A former staffer at *Report on Business* magazine, he has written features and reviews for numerous publications, including the *Toronto Star*, *National Post*, the *Walrus* and *Toronto Life*. Al-Solaylee holds a Ph.D. from the University of Nottingham and has taught at the University of Waterloo and York University. He lives in Toronto.